Day Trading for Beginners

*Proven Strategies to Succeed and Create Passive Income
in the Stock Market - Introduction to Forex Swing
Trading, Options, Futures & ETFs*

Table of Contents

Introduction

Thank you for purchasing this beginner's guide to day trading.

In this book, you will learn the fundamentals of day trading and how it is different from other investment opportunities. You will also learn important trading strategies that many profitable day traders are using today.

This book is written in a simple and straightforward style so even people with no prior background in the stock market can easily learn the 'secrets of the trade'. If you are a newbie in day trading, this book can equip you with a basic understanding of where to begin, how to start, what to expect, and how you can create your own strategy.

However, merely reading this book will not make you a profitable day trader. Making money in the stock market hardly comes from reading a book. As you will learn later, revenue comes from actually doing it. Knowing is not enough. You need to practice, use the right tools, and continuously invest in your own education.

Even those with some years of experience in day trading can still benefit from this book's discussion of traditional strategies that most day traders are using effectively. Even if you are not a novice reader, I still encourage you to read the whole book as you may still find valuable lessons in these pages.

Day trading can help you make money, but it is not a sure way to get rich fast. This is not similar to playing the lottery. This is the biggest misconception that people have about day trading, and hopefully, you will dispel this notion after you read this book.

In fact, around 95% of people who start day trading end up in net loss.[1] It is easy to be part of the 95%. It is easy to lose money in day trading. So remember this number one rule in day trading:

Rule No. 1 - Day Trading Is Not a Get-Rich-Quick Scheme

A lot of people think that it is easy to make money in day trading. After all, you just need to buy some stocks, wait for them to go higher a bit, and then you sell them for a good price, right? Unfortunately, this is not true. If that is the case, then everyone would be rich by now.

You should always remember that day trading is not easy and it will not make you a millionaire overnight.

If you have this misconception, and you want to get rich fast, you must stop reading this book and invest your money somewhere else. If you are not ready to lose money in day trading, then forget day trading.

Day trading is a highly competitive market. Day traders are always trying to make a profit by outsmarting other day traders. The primary goal of day trading is to grab money from other day traders while they are also trying to take your money.

This is the reason why this is an intellectually intense financial activity. Basically, you can't make money in the stock market. The only reason there's money in the stock market is that other traders have invested it there. The money that you want to take belongs to other traders and they will do everything to hold on to their money.

Day trading is not easy peasy. And in light of this, you should remember rule number two.

Rule No. 2 - Day Trading Is Hard

Day trading is a serious business, and you must treat it as such. You can be profitable in day trading only if you have the capacity and the perseverance to pursue this opportunity. Trading on high emotions is the number one reason why day traders fail.

You have to practice self-discipline and manage your money well. Decent day traders take care of their capital as carefully as astronauts monitor their oxygen supply. In day trading, you can't be weak. You need to be above average if not excellent in order to win the game.

Sadly, day trading usually attracts gamblers or impulsive people who feel they are entitled. If you have this sense of entitlement, then this book is not for you. Day trading is not fit for you. You must have the mindset of a winner. You need to think like a winner. Feel like a winner. Act like a winner.

Changing your mindset is not easy. But if you wish to be profitable in this business, you must work on changing and developing your personality. In order to succeed in day trading, you need discipline, knowledge, and motivation. These elements, in fact, will make you successful in any profession you choose.

Remember, day trading is a profession. People who are serious in this financial activity treat it like they would treat work in medicine, engineering, or law. Day trading requires the right education, discipline, and practice.

You need to dedicate countless hours reading about different trading styles, observing how successful traders are doing the job, and practicing using simulation programs so you can learn how to trade in the real arena.

Many successful day traders are now making $500 to $1,000 every day. This is equivalent to $10,000 to $20,000 each month or roughly $120,000 to $240,000 per year.

Day trading can pay you well. However, it is not easy money. Similar to engineers, lawyers, or doctors who are required to study long years and dedicate their talents in their profession, day traders also have to spend time studying the industry and perform well.

Many people are enticed to try day trading mainly because of their lifestyle. It is possible to work from home, spend only a few hours every day, and go wherever you want to go whenever you want.

You can easily spend more time with your family and friends without waiting for your scheduled vacation or requesting from your manager or boss. In day trading, you are your own boss. Because day trading is a business, you are the executive of your own business, so you make your own decisions.

Ultimately, once you master day trading skills, you can easily make thousands of dollars every day, which is a lot more than most other careers pay. There even are traders who make $2,000 every day or more.

Regardless of your location, $2,000 per day is a significant amount of money that can change your life. If you want to control how you want and how much you make, day trading is an easy way to begin.

Let's compare day trading with opening a restaurant. If you want to go into the food business, you need to spend a huge amount of money on inventory, rent, equipment, people, training, licenses, insurance, marketing, and a whole lot more. And you still won't be guaranteed to earn money from this business. Many businesses are like this.

On the other hand, day trading is quite easy to set up and start. You can sign up for a trading account today, usually at no cost, then begin trading tomorrow. Of course, you need to understand the fundamentals of day trading, at least, before you start. However, the logistics of starting day trading are quite easy if you compare it to other businesses and professions.

Another advantage of day trading is the ease of managing the cash flow. You can purchase a stock, and if things don't turn out well, you can easily sell it. Compare this to people who have to manage inventory from different suppliers.

There are many things that can go wrong when you are getting your supplies so you can sell food in your restaurant. You may need to deal with different problems with customer satisfaction, quality, marketing, distribution, shipping, and vendors. Plus, your money is locked in for the whole process. Unless everything goes well, you can hardly do anything about it. There are instances that you may not even accept a small loss and you just want to go out of business.

If things are not going well with day trading, you can easily come out as quickly as clicking a simple button. It is easy to start over in day trading, and this is a highly attractive element of any business.

Closing your day trading business is also quite easy. If you realize that day trading is not for you, or if you have not succeeded in making money from it, you can easily stop the business, close your accounts, and withdraw your balances. Apart from the money and the time that you have already spent, there are or other charges or fees that you have to pay.

Closing other forms of business is not nearly as easy, It will take a lot of requirements before you can close your store, lay off your people, or walk away from your rental contract.

Why then are people losing money in day trading? Later in this book, we will explain the specific reasons behind this critical question. But more often than not, the most common reason why people fail in day trading is that they don't consider it as a serious business.

Instead, they consider it as a form of gambling, which will quickly and easily make them rich. Some people begin to day trade as a hobby or for fun because they consider it as cool. They trade for the adventure and excitement of short-term gambling in the stock market. They play around in the market, but they don't commit to learning the fundamentals of day trading.

They may be fortunate a few times and make some money, but in the end, the market will punish them. If you are new in day trading, you should never lose sight of the fact that you are actually competing with professionals and experienced traders around the world. Many of these seasoned traders are masters of the trade, and they are equipped with the tools that help them make profitable trading decisions.

You must always remember the second rule - day trading is a business, and you must take it seriously. You must wake up early each day, prepare yourself on the stocks that you want to trade, and make sure that your tools are ready before the market opens.

If you have a restaurant business, can you open your shop three hours late? You can't close the restaurant just because you are not in the mood, you are not feeling well, or you didn't have the time to restock ingredients for your crew to prepare meals. You should always be ready.

This should also be the case with day trading. You need to be educated, you need to use the right tools, and you must hustle every day.

Day trading can be a lucrative business if you are willing to do whatever it takes to succeed.

Chapter 1 - How Day Trading Works

In this chapter, we will take a look at the fundamentals of day trading so you will understand what day trading is, and how it works.

We will also cover some of the basic tools and strategies that you can use to be profitable in the business. As with any profession, tools are useless if you don't know how to properly use them. This book is written to guide you on the proper use of these tools.

Day Trading Vs. Swing Trading

A basic question to start with is this one - what are you looking for as a day trader? The answer here is quite easy.

First, you must look for stocks that are following a predictable trend. Then, you need to trade them in one single day. You don't need to keep them longer than a day. If you purchase stocks of Amazon (AMZN) today, you should not hold the stocks overnight and sell them tomorrow. It is no longer day trading if you hold on to your position. That one is called swing trading.

As a day trader, you need to understand the difference between day trading and swing trading. The latter is a type of trading in which you hold the stocks over a certain period of time, usually from one day to several weeks. This is a different style of trading, and you must not use these tools and strategies that are ideal for day trading if you want to follow the swing trading style.

Remember, day trading is a business (Rule 2). Swing trading is also a business, albeit a totally different type of business. The differences between day trading and swing trading are similar to the differences between owning a meat processing plant and a hamburger chain.

Both businesses involve food, but these are not similar. They operate with different revenue models, market segments, regulations, and time frames. You must not confuse day trading with other trading styles just because the trades are performed in the stock market.

Professional day traders close their positions before the stock market closes. Many traders perform both swing trading and day trading. They are aware that they are running two different businesses, and they are trained to manage the risks of these two types of trading.

One of the main differences between swing trading and day trading is the style of choosing stocks. Many traders do not day trade and swing trade the same stocks. Swing traders often look for stocks in established companies that they know will not lose their value in a few weeks.

But for day trading, you can trade any stock you want including companies that are predicted to go bankrupt. Day traders don't care what happens to the stocks after the market closes.

As a matter of fact, many of the companies that you day trade are quite risky to hold overnight because they may lose much of their value in a short period of time.

At this point, you are now ready to know the third rule of day trading:

Rule No. 3 - Do Not Hold Stocks Overnight

Even if you will sell at a loss, it is still ideal not to hold on to any position overnight.

Buy Long, Sell Short

In day trading, you buy stocks in the hope that their price will increase later in the day. This is known as buying long or just long. Whenever you hear a trader saying "I'm long 200 shares MSFT," it means that he bought 200 shares of Microsoft and would like to sell them at a higher price.

If the market is going higher, going long is good. But what will you do with the stocks if the prices are plummeting? In this case, you can sell the stocks short and still make some money.

Day traders may borrow shares from their broker and place them in the market, hoping that the price will go lower and that they can buy the shares at a lower price and make a profit. This is known as selling short, or just short.

When you hear a trader say "I am short Microsoft," it means he has sold short Microsoft stocks and he hopes that the price will drop. If the price is going lower, you owe 100 shares to your broker, which is usually deducted from your day trading account. This means you need to return the shares back to your broker. Most brokers want shares instead of money.

Therefore, if the price decreases, you can purchase them at an affordable rate than your purchase price and make some money. Let's say that you borrow 100 shares of Microsoft from your broker, and you sell them at $150 per share. Apple's price then plummets to $140, so you buy back the 100 shares at 140 and return them to the broker.

In this transaction, you have made $1,000 ($10 per share). What if the Microsoft stocks go up to $160? In this case, you need to buy 100 shares and give them back to your broker, because you owe them shares and not cash. Hence, you need to buy 100 shares at $160 so you can return 100 shares to your broker. This means you have lost $1000.

Short-sellers make money if the price of the stock they have borrowed and sold falls down. This type of trading is essential because the prices of the stocks normally drop much faster than they increase. Remember, fear is stronger than greed. Hence, short-sellers, when they trade right, can make a lot of money while other traders go into a panic mode and begin to sell their shares.

But just like anything in the market that has the potential for profit, short selling can be also risky. In buying company stocks for $10, the worst thing that can happen is that the company files for bankruptcy that same day and you lose $10. There's a limit to your loss, but if you short sell that company for $10 and then the price, instead of falling down, begins to go higher, then there's no limit to your loss.

Let's say the price increases from $10 to $100. Your broker will demand you to return the shares. You may lose all your money in your trading account, and your broker may even file a legal case against you to recover money if your funds are insufficient.

Short selling is considered legal and helpful in the stock market because of the following:

- *It provides the stock market with valuable information* - Day traders usually perform comprehensive due diligence to learn facts and flaws that support their assumption that a particular company is overvalued. Without short selling, the stock prices can go higher and higher, even if the company is not doing well.

- ***Short sellers balance the market*** - Short selling is necessary to keep the stock market alive. If the price is predicted to go lower, you might be wondering why the broker permitted you to short sell rather than selling the stocks themselves prior to the price drop. Remember, brokers, are usually interested in holding their position for the long-term. Through short-selling, investors will be able to generate extra profit by lending their shares.

Also, take note that long-term investors who make their shares available for short-selling are not afraid of short-term ups and downs. They usually have good reasons why they have invested in the company, and they are not usually interested in selling their stocks in a short period of time.

Therefore, they prefer to lend their stocks to traders who wish to make money from short-term market fluctuations. In exchange for lending their stocks, they will charge interest. So, by short selling, they will need to pay some interest to your broker as the cost of borrowing these shares.

Brokers don't usually charge interest if you short sell within the same day. On the other hand, swing traders who sell short typically have to pay daily interest on the stocks they borrowed.

In general, short selling is a risky practice in day trading. For example, some traders are long-biased because they are more interested in buying stocks that they want to sell for a higher rate.

Most profitable day traders don't have any bias. They will short sell when they think that the shares are ready. They will also buy whenever it fits their trade strategy. You need to be careful when you short stocks.

Many of the strategies that you will learn in this book are applicable for holding long positions. There are also strategies that are only recommended for short selling.

Institutional vs. Retail Traders

Retail traders are individuals who can be either part-time or full traders but don't work for a firm, and are not managing funds from other people. These traders hold a small percentage of the volume in the trade market.

On the other hand, institutional traders are composed of hedge funds, mutual funds, and investment banks who are often armed with advanced software, and are usually engaged in high-frequency trading.

Nowadays, human involvement is quite minimal in the operations of investment firms. Backed up by professional analysts and huge investments, institutional investors can be quite aggressive.

So at this point, you might be wondering how a beginner like you can compete against the big players?

Our advantage is the freedom and flexibility we enjoy. Institutional traders have the legal obligation to trade. Meanwhile, individual traders are free to trade or to take a break from trading if the market is currently unstable.

Institutional traders should be active in the market and trade huge volumes of stocks regardless of the stock price. Individual traders are free to sit out and trade if there are possible opportunities in the market.

But sadly, most retail traders do not possess the know-how in identifying the right time to be active and the best time to wait. If you want to be profitable in day trading, you need to eliminate greed and develop patience.

The biggest problem of losers in day trading is not the size of their accounts or the lack of access to technology, but their sheer lack of discipline. Many are prone to bad money management and over-trading.

Some retail traders are successful by following the guerilla strategy, which refers to the unconventional approach to trading derived from guerilla warfare. Guerilla combatants are skilled in using hit-and-run tactics like raids, sabotage, and ambushes to manipulate a bigger and less-mobile conventional opponent.

The US military is considered as one of the strongest armies in the modern world. But this mighty force suffered humiliation caused by the guerilla warfare used by North Vietnam during the Vietnam War.

Following this analogy, guerilla trading involves waiting or hiding until you are ready to grab an opportunity to win small battles in the financial warfare. This can help you gain fast revenue while minimizing your risk.

Remember, your mission is not to defeat institutional traders. Instead, you should focus on waiting for the right opportunity to earn your target income.

As a retail trader, you can make profits from market volatility. It can be impossible to make money if the markets are flat. Only institutional traders have the tools, expertise, and money to gamble in such circumstances.

You must learn how to choose stocks that can help you make fast decisions to the downside or upside in a predictable approach. On the other hand, institutional traders follow high frequency trading, which allows them to profit from very small price movements. Some savvy retail traders often stay away from stocks that are heavily traded by institutional traders.

As a retail trader, you should only work in the retail domain. It is usually a loss if you trade other stocks that other retail traders are not seeing or trading. The advantage of retail trading is that other retail traders also use them. The more traders use these strategies, the better they can work.

As more traders learn effective stock market strategies, more people will join the market so more stocks will move up faster. The more players in the market, the faster it will move. This is the reason why it is important for successful traders to share their strategies. This will not only help other traders to become more profitable, but it can also increase the number of traders who are using proven strategies.

There's no benefit in hiding these strategies or keeping them secret. In computer-aided trading, most of the stocks will follow the trend of the market, unless there's a good reason not to follow. Therefore, when the market is rising, most stocks will also move up. If the overall market is declining, the prices of the stocks will also decline.

But you should also bear in mind that there will be a handful of stocks that can go against the grain because they have a catalyst. These are known as Alpha Predators, which we will discuss in more detail in Chapter 4.

But for a brief overview, Alpha Predators are what retail traders are hunting for. These stocks usually tank when the markets are running, and they run when the markets are tanking.

It is generally okay if the market is running, and the stocks are running as well. Just be sure that you are trading stocks that are moving because they have a valid reason to move, and are not just moving with the general market conditions.

Probably, you are wondering what the basic catalyst for stocks is to make them ideal for day trading.

Here are some catalysts:

- Debt offerings
- Buybacks
- Stock splits
- Management changes
- Layoffs
- Restructuring
- Major contract wins / losses

- Partnerships / alliances

- Major product releases

- Mergers and / or acquisitions

- FDA approval / disapproval

- Earnings surprises

- Earnings reports

Retail traders who are engaged in reversal trades usually choose stocks that are selling off because there has been some bad press about the company. Whenever there's a fast sell-off because of bad press, many traders will notice and begin monitoring the stock for what is called a bottom reversal.

It can be difficult to perform a reversal trade if the stocks are trending down with the overall market like what happened to oil several years ago. The stock value increases by 20 cents and you may think it is a reversal. Then they are quickly sold off for another 60 cents. The sell-off is happening because the stocks are getting bad press.

For a while, oil was a weak sector and the majority of the energy and oil stocks were selling off. If a sector is weak, then it is not a good time for a reversal trade. This is where you need to identify the reason behind any significant movement in the market.

In order to do that, you need to remember the fourth rule in day trading:

Rule No. 4 - Always ask: is this stock moving because the general market is moving, or there's a unique catalyst behind this movement?

Research is crucial at this point. As you gain experience as a day trader, you will need to identify the difference between general market trends and catalyst-based movements. As a day trader, you need to be careful that you are not on the wrong side of the trade, and going against institutional traders.

How can you do that? Rather than trying to emulate institutional traders, you need to detect where the retail traders are hanging out on a particular day, and then place your bet with them.

Stay away from trading stocks that are not getting enough attention. You will be in a sandbox doing your own thing. Go where everyone else is going. Concentrate on the stocks that are moving every day and are getting attention from retail traders.

Are blue-chip stocks like IBM, Coca-Cola, or Apple ideal for retail traders? You can try, but you need to remember that these are slow-paced stocks, which are heavily dominated by algorithmic traders and institutional traders. Plus, they are often very hard to trade.

How can you identify the stocks that are alluring retail traders? There are some proven ways to do this.

First, you can use day trading stock scanners. Later in this book, we will discuss how you can set up your own day trading scanner. Basically, the stocks that are significantly moving up or down are the stocks that are being monitored by retail traders.

Second, find online community groups or social media groups where retail traders hang out. Twitter and StockTwits are often good places to learn what is currently trending. If you regularly follow successful traders, then you may see for yourself what everyone is following. There's a big advantage to being part of a community of day traders.

You can read the insights of traders and the specific stocks they are considering. If you are a lone trader, then you may be out of touch in the market. You will just make it difficult for yourself because you will not know where the action is.

A Day in the Life of a Day Trader

Steve is a day trader who lives in New York. His day usually starts at around 6 am with pre-market scanning. As early as

6 am, he already knows what stocks are gapping up or down. He scans the market to check if there's volume in the market.

Then Steve begins browsing the news for possible catalysts that might be behind the gap. He begins to set up an alert list. He rules out some stocks, and then chooses which ones he is interested to trade or not. By 9 am, he is chatting with his fellow day traders as they go over his list. By 9:30 AM, when the stock market opens, he is ready to execute his plan.

In the New York Stock Exchange (NYSW), the heaviest volumes happen between 9:30 am and 11:30 am, which is also the most volatile period in the market. This is the best window for trading and performing momentum trading, which you will later learn in this book.

Liquidity is the main advantage of having all that volume in the market. When the volume is high, it only means there are many buyers and sellers in the market. After lunch, you can have good trading patterns, but the volume starts to fade. Liquidity is also affected, so it can be difficult to get in and out of stocks. This is particularly crucial to consider when you want to take bigger shares.

Steve's focus is to always trade near the market's opening. He only trades within the first one or two hours of the market opening. He rarely trades during midday, and on a good day, he reaches his trading goal by 8 am.

After lunch, Steve has reached his goal and he would now be waiting out unless there's a significant movement in the market. By late afternoon, he reviews his trades for the day.

Today, Steve made $2,000 by 1 pm. What is he going to do? Will he walk away with that money or will he keep trading until he starts losing this money? He decided to call it a day and cash out.

Steve usually finishes his trading by lunchtime, and then he is off his way to doing whatever he likes. But whenever he loses money before lunch, he would continue fighting to stay in the market. He would keep on trading trying to regain his money.

As such, mid-day trading is often dominated by traders who have lost their money in the morning and are now trying to gain their losses.

This causes high volatility, which is not a good sign as it may cause stocks to become unpredictable because people are moving a lot of stocks. This is usually the time of the day that is often dominated by amateur traders.

Steve avoids pre-market trading because there's minimal liquidity as there is very few day traders during this period. This means stocks can increase a few points higher then suddenly drop. It is impossible to get in and out with these shares.

The great advantage for Steve is that he can be done trading before most of the people are even awake. Then he can spend the rest of his day at his own leisure or focusing on his other businesses. He tries to hit his daily goal early on and then relax. He is aware of the fact that it is quite easy to lose money in the stock market, so once he has made some money, he stops trading.

Chapter 2 - Managing Risk in Day Trading

There are three important components of day trading that you need to master so you can become successful in this business:

1. Sound Psychology

2. Effective Day Trading Strategies

3. Risk Management

These three are the pillars of day trading. If you are weak in one area, the whole business can collapse. It is a common beginner's mistake to concentrate only on trading strategies. An effective strategy delivers positive expectancy because it produces higher profits than losses over a certain period of time.

All the day trading strategies that you will learn in this book are used by profitable traders, but they should be properly executed. Bear in mind that even the most effective strategy cannot guarantee success in every trade.

No single strategy can guarantee you of never having a losing trade or even experiencing a series of losses. This is the reason risk control should be an important part of every trading strategy.

The number one reason new traders fail at day trading is their inability to manage risks. We have the tendency to accept revenue fast and we also like to wait around until losing trades return to even.

By the time some amateur traders learn how to manage their risks, their accounts are depleted. To become successful in this craft, you should learn risk management rules, and then properly execute them.

There must be a clear rule that can guide you when you should get out of the trade. It is okay to commit mistakes in your trade. In fact, even ultra-successful traders still make bad decisions despite their experience.

You will lose a lot of trades, but don't forget to be a good loser. You need to accept a loss. This is an important part of day trading. In the strategies outlined in this book, you will learn the entry points, the exit targets, and the stop loss.

As a beginner, you should follow the rules and plans of your trading strategy. And this is one of the challenges that you need to face whenever you are in a bad trade.

Many amateur day traders justify their decision to hold bad stocks by saying, "Well, it's Amazon, and it's a billion dollar company. Surely, they will not get out of business, so I think

I will hold just a bit longer." You should not do this. You should follow the rules of your own day trading strategy. You can easily return to the trade, but it can be difficult to recover from a huge loss.

Get out once you are losing money, then promptly return once the market is showing stability. Each time you trade, you are exposing your money, so you need to minimize this risk exposure. You must find the ideal set-up, then manage the risk with the proper share size and stop loss.

Here's the fifth rule in day trading:

Rule No. 5 - Risk Management is important for successful day trading.

An ideal setup is an opportunity for you to get into a trade with minimal risk. This means you might risk $50 but you have the potential to make $150. This is a 3:10 profit-loss ratio.

Meanwhile, if you get into a setup where you are risking $50 to make $5, then you have a less than 1 risk-reward ratio, and this is a trade that you should avoid. Seasoned day traders will not take the trades with profit-to-loss ratio of less than 2:1.

This means if you buy $500 stocks and you are risking $50 on it, you should sell it for at least $600 to make at least $100.

Certainly, if the price comes down to $400, you should accept the loss and exit the market with only $400 ($50 loss).

If you are not able to find a good setup with the ideal profit-to-loss ratio, then try to move on and keep looking for another trade. As a day trader, you should always look for opportunities to obtain low risk entries with huge win potential.

Part of the learning process in day trading is the ability to identify setups that have huge potential for winning. As a newbie in this area, you may find it difficult to identify different setups. It can be difficult for you to identify a false breakout from a home run. This is something that you can develop through experience and training. We will discuss this in more detail in the succeeding chapters.

Using a 2:1 win-loss ratio, there's a chance that you can be wrong 40% of the time, but you can still make money. Again, your job as a day trader is to manage risk, not merely to buy and sell stocks. Your chosen broker will handle the transaction of buying and selling. Your main responsibility is to manage the risks.

Whenever you buy stocks, you are exposing money to a risk. How can you manage this? Basically, there are three steps you need to remember in order to manage risk. You need to determine if you are trading the right stock.

Later in Chapter 4, we will learn how to find the right stocks for day trading. We will discuss in detail how to find stocks that are ideal for day traders, and what criteria you must look for in them.

Basically, you must remember the following:

- Avoid stocks that are mainly traded by institutional traders and algorithmic traders.

- Avoid stocks that have a small relative trading volume.

- Avoid penny stocks that are clearly manipulated.

- Avoid stocks that are moving without clear basic catalysts.

You will learn more about this in Chapter 4. Bear in mind that risk management begins from selecting the right type of stock to trade. You can have the best platform and tools, and become skilled in day trading strategies. But you will certainly lose money if you are trading the wrong stocks.

You also need to determine the ideal share size you should take. Are 10 shares enough? Is it recommended to take 100 shares? How about 1000 shares? This all depends on the size of your account as well as your daily target.

If you are targeting $1,000 per day, then 10 to 20 shares will suffice. You can either increase your account size or take more shares. You may need to lower your daily goal if you don't have enough money to trade for a $1,000 daily target.

I am holding around $25,000 in my trading account and I usually choose 800 shares to trade. My daily goal is $500 or $120,000/year. That is sufficient for my lifestyle.

What is your trading goal? What is your stop loss?

The absolute maximum a trader should risk on any trade is 2% of his or her account equity. For example, if you have a $30,000 account, you should not risk more than $600 per trade, and if you have a $10,000 account, you should not risk more than $200.

If you have a small account, it is best to trade fewer shares at first. When you see an attractive trade but you need to place a logical stop where higher than 2% of your capital is at risk, then you should pass on that trade, and move on to find another one.

Always know your risk tolerance, and many profitable traders don't risk more than 2% of their capital on a single trade.

Three Steps in Managing Risks

Here are the three steps you can take to effectively manage your risks:

Step 1 - Figure out the maximum dollar risk for the trade you are planning

Take note that this should not be higher than the 2% of your account. Make sure that you have calculated this before you start your trading day.

For example, let's say that you have a $20,000 account. With the 2% rule, you can only risk $400 for a single trade. If you want to be more conservative, you can limit yourself to trading $200 every trade or 1% of your account.

Step 2 - Estimate your max risk per share and stop-loss strategy

We will discuss this in more detail in Chapter 6, wherein for each strategy, we explore what the stop loss must be.

Let's say that you are looking at the stock of BBRY (Blackberry) using ABCD Pattern Strategy. You buy stocks at $8 and want to sell it at $11, with a stop loss at $6.50. You will be risking $1.50 / share.

Step 3 - Find the absolute maximum number of shares you should trade each time

You can do this by dividing 1 by 2. Following the examples above, you will be allowed to buy only 133 shares or rounded to 125 shares.

With the strategies explained in Chapter 6, you will learn where the stop loss should be based on your trade plan and technical analysis.

You can only consider max loss for your account depending on your account size. So you need to make that call for yourself. For instance, if your stop is higher than your moving average, you need to make some calculations and check if this stop is bigger than the maximum account size.

If the break of moving average will yield a $300 loss, and you have set a $200 max loss every trade, then you must cancel the trade or take a lower number of shares.

You may think that it can be difficult to compute share size or stop loss depending on a max loss on your account, while you are waiting for the right opportunity. It's true that you need to make fast decisions or you may lose the opportunity. It is also true that computing your stop loss and max loss in your account size in a live trade is not usually easy.

Let me take you back to Rule No. 2: Day Trading Is Hard.

You need to practice, and it is ideal for amateur traders to practice under supervision for at least three months in a simulated account. Through this, you can learn how to manage your account as well as your risk for every trade. Gradually, you can easily figure out the numbers by yourself.

Risk Management and Trading Psychology

Day trading is often difficult and a lot of new traders fail. It requires sound decision-making skills, as well as strong self-discipline.

When you learned that an investor has taken a stake in Tesla, your initial reaction might be to join the trend. However, you need to make a fast decision whether you must buy or sell or sell short Tesla stocks. You can effectively do this with discipline.

Your trading strategies will gradually improve over time. But as early as now, you should understand that the key to making money in day trading is to control yourself, and practice self-discipline.

It can be difficult to predict the stock market behavior, and if you don't know what you will do, you can lose the game.

You need to stand on your own feet as even the most advanced trading tools cannot help a trader who doesn't know what to do. You need to ask the following questions:

- Does this particular course of action fit into my trading strategy?

- What trading strategy will this action fit into?

- If this trade goes awry, where do I stop?

- How much money am I risking in the trade, and what is the potential reward?

This is what many day traders find difficult. The decision-making process in day trading is usually a tough multitasking call. On top of that, you may feel the pressure. Many day traders, even successful ones, still find themselves looking at their screens and can't even figure out what action to take.

This type of paralysis is not uncommon when you are under pressure. When this happens, you must understand that you might have pushed yourself a bit too far out of your comfort zone. It can happen even to the most experienced day trader, albeit only once in a while.

By trading regularly, you will gain some experience, and it's ideal to work on the edge of your comfort zone so you can push your boundaries. But if you find yourself too far outside of your comfort zone and beyond your risk tolerance, you may end up making some costly errors. It is always best to foster a self-awareness.

Learn how to be calm under pressure, so you can make decisions without losing your mind. Regularly assess your decisions and always review your performance.

Are you making profits in your trades? Are you getting winning streaks or losing streaks? If you are losing five trades in a row, are you checking your emotions and maintaining your composure? Or will you let your judgment cloud your mind?

Discipline is crucial to develop your trading muscles, which require exercise to grow. Once you have developed these muscles, you need to exercise regularly so you can maintain your physique.

Day trading can give you this opportunity. Regularly exercise your ability to demonstrate discipline and self-control. Some of these skills are also comparable to learning to drive a car. Once you have acquired this skill, no one can take it away.

When you've learned it, the skill of identifying a great stock chart will not fade away. However, discipline is something that you need to regularly work at to be a profitable trader.

You have chosen a venture in which constant learning is important. This profession can be invigorating. But take note that if you begin to gain too much confidence, and think you have outsmarted the market on trading know-how, or that there is no need to learn anymore, you will surely get a quick reminder from the stock market.

You may lose money, and you shall see that the market can rectify your overconfidence. The ability to make fast decisions and your ability to make and then follow your rules for day trading are important for success in this market.

As you read this guide, you can learn more about risk management. Everything that you do as a day trader comes back to managing risks because, at the end of the day, this is the most important concept for you to understand.

Visualize yourself as a risk manager. You need to effectively manage risks so that you can make good decisions even under extreme pressure. This leads us to Rule No. 6 in day trading:

Rule No. 6 - Your Broker Will Trade the Stocks for You

Your focus is to manage risk. It can be quite difficult to become a successful day trader without effective risk management skills, even if you are knowledgeable with many trading strategies.

Day traders are in the business of day trading. You must clearly define your risk as a business person. You must specifically know the amount of money you are willing to risk on any single trade.

As mentioned earlier in this chapter, the acceptable risk depends on the size of your trading account as well as your trading method, personality, as well as risk tolerance. But you should remember the 2% rule discussed above. This rule is very important that we need to highlight it again: the maximum amount that you can risk on any trade should not exceed 2% of your account size.

For instance, if you have a $60,000 account, you should not risk more than $1200 per trade. If you have a $20,000 account, you should never risk more than $400 per trade.

If your account is still small, you should limit yourself to trading fewer shares. If you think there's a good trade, but a logical step is to place where more than 2% of your equity is at risk, sit it out and move on. You may have minimal risk, but you should never risk more.

Again, never risk more than 2% of your day trading account.

Chapter 3 - Hunting for Stocks to Trade

After risk management, the next challenge for a day trader is looking for stocks to trade. You may spend a lot of time studying the mechanism behind day trading, but when it comes to choosing stocks, it can be quite difficult. You will certainly experience this as a new trader.

Apex Predators

Bear in mind that not all stocks are ideal for day trading as it only works on stocks with high relative volume. Some stocks such as AAPL will usually trade millions of shares every day, while other stocks may only trade a couple of hundreds of thousands.

So does this mean you should only trade Apple stocks? The volume for a stock is relative. And focusing on the total volume is not enough. There are some stocks that on average will trade with such high volume. You must look for what is above average for that particular stock.

For example, 35 million shares of Apple traded in a single day could be the average. Avoid trading this stock unless it hits double. If the volume is not higher than usual, it could mean that the market is dominated by institutional traders and algorithmic investors. Move on to the next.

Bear in mind that high relative volume stocks are independent of what their sector and overall market are following. If the market is weak, it only means that most stocks are selling off. It doesn't matter if the stocks are Amazon, Facebook, or Google. If the market is strong, the price of most stocks will rise. Likewise, if you learn that the market is bearish, the overall market is collapsing because the whole market is losing its value and not only certain stocks.

This is also true with particular sectors. For instance, if the energy sector is weak, it means all energy companies are losing their value as a group.

But how can you detect the market behavior? Index funds like S&P 500 or Dow Jones are often good indicators of what the overall market is doing. If the S&P and Dow Jones are weak, then the general market is collapsing.

The behavior of stocks with high relative volume is independent of the general market. Every day, only a few stocks are traded independently of their sector and the general market. Retail traders only trade those stocks that are known as Apex Predators.

In the Animal Kingdom, Apex Predators are predators located at the top of the food chain. No one preys upon them. In the world of day trading, Apex Predator stocks are those that are not dependent on the general market and their sector. They are not controlled by the market.

Therefore, the next rule is about Apex Predators:

Rule No. 7 - Day Traders Only Trade Apex Predators

Profitable day traders also trade high relative volume stocks that have fundamental catalysts and are traded regardless of the condition in the overall market.

What makes a stock an Apex Predator? Normally, it is the release of fundamental news about the stock either the day prior to or during the same trading day. Essential news or events for companies can have huge effects on their value in the market and thus serve as fundamental catalysts for the price action.

As enumerated in Chapter 1, some examples of basic catalysts for stocks that make them ideal for day trading include the following:

- Debt offerings
- Buybacks
- Stock splits
- Management changes

- Layoffs

- Restructuring

- Major contract wins / losses

- Partnerships / alliances

- Major product releases

- Mergers and / or acquisitions

- FDA approval / disapproval

- Earnings surprises

- Earnings reports

In Chapter 6, we will explore specific day trading strategies such as Moving Averages, VWAP Strategy, Reversal, and Momentum.

At this point, your only concern should be how you can find the stock for each strategy. Day traders usually categorize stocks for retail trading into three groups. Through this, you can gain some clarity on how you can hunt for stocks and what strategy you must use.

There are other methods of categorizing stocks for day trading, and even some day traders do not agree with this method of classification. Therefore, before I discuss the three categories, it is important to explain first the definition of market capitalization and "float".

In day trading, when we say float, it means the number of shares available for trading.

Microsoft, for instance, as of November 2019, has 7.3 billion shares in the market that are available for trade. The company is deemed as a "Mega Cap" type of stock. Such stocks often don't move so much during the day because you need a huge sum of money to move the volume.

Hence, Microsoft shares usually move by a few dollars every day. Mega Cap stocks are not volatile, so retail traders don't like to trade them. As a day trader, you should always look for volatility.

Meanwhile, there are some stocks that have a very low float. For instance, Nortech Systems (ticker: NYSYS) has only 981,000 stocks available for trade. This means that the supply of stocks of NYSYS is low and so a big demand can easily move the share price.

Low float stocks are volatile and can move quite fast. Usually, low float stocks are priced under $10 because they are early IPO companies that are still not profitable. These companies are still growing, and by growing further, they issue more stocks and raise more money from the public, and gradually increase their market capitalization.

Low float stocks are called micro cap stocks or small cap stocks. Retail traders love low float stocks.

Now, let's go back to the three classes mentioned earlier.

Low Float Stocks

The first class is composed of low float stocks that are priced under $10. These stocks are quite volatile, moving from 10% to as high as 1,000% every day. With this extreme volatility, you should be cautious when dealing with these stocks.

Just as you can grow your $1,000 into $10,000 in one trade, you can also diminish your $1,000 to only 10 in a few minutes. Low float stocks under $10 are also usually manipulated and usually not easy to trade. And so, only experienced day traders must venture in these stocks.

Rare is the chance that amateur day traders can trade low float stocks with such efficiency and accuracy. If you try to trade low float stocks that are under $10, then the risk is high that you will turn your $1000 into nothing in a few days. For a low float stock, the Bull Flag Momentum Strategy (which you will learn in Chapter 6) is highly recommended. Other day trading strategies explored in this book are not recommended for low float stocks under $10.

In general, you cannot sell short low float stocks that are priced under $10. Bear in mind that in order to short sell, you must borrow shares from your stockbroker, which is highly unlikely for volatile stocks.

Even if your broker approves your loan, I highly implore you not to try short selling low float stocks. They are extremely volatile and you may end up losing all your money, and even come out negative because you have to pay your broker.

Remember, you can become a fulltime profitable day trader even without having to short-sell risky stocks. If you are just a beginner in this field, sit this one out and try it if you have gained some experience in the field.

Medium Float Stocks

The second category of stocks is called medium float stocks. It is in the range of $10 to $100. These stocks have medium floats between 5 million to 500 million shares.

Many of the strategies discussed in this book can work well on these stocks, especially the Resistance Strategies. These are Medium float stocks priced more than $100 and are not ideal for day traders.

More often than not, you can't buy many shares of medium float stocks because of their high price. Thus, it is fundamentally futile to day trade them.

Mega Cap Stocks

The third category of stocks for trading is mega cap stocks such as Home Depot, Microsoft, Yahoo, Ali Baba, and Apple. These are strong companies that usually have more than $500 million in outstanding shares available for buying and selling.

Mega stocks are traded in millions of shares each day, and they only move if huge institutional traders, hedge funds, and investment banks are trading large positions.

Day traders who usually trade between 100 and 1,000 shares cannot cause any significant movement in these stocks. Day traders must stay away from these stocks unless there's a good catalyst behind the move.

In the strategies described in Chapter 6, Moving Average and Reversal Strategies often work well on mega stocks.

But remember, unless there's a catalyst, these stocks are heavily traded by algorithms and high frequency traders, and are not ideal for day trading.

Chapter 4 - Day Trading Tools and Platforms

Just like starting any other business or profession, you need a few important tools to begin day trading. Basically, you need a broker and a platform to execute your orders. These are the tools that you will certainly need to function as a day trader.

As explained in Chapter 3, you also need a stock scanner to help you find a watch list, and look for potential setups in real time. On top of a stock scanner, it is ideal to be part of a trading community.

Day Trading Broker

You need a reliable broker for day trading. You don't need a popular broker; you need a reliable one. Remember, your broker is your vehicle to trade. Even if you are trading properly, you can lose money if you have a bad broker.

There are numerous brokers out there with different software and price schemes. Some are cheap but terrible, and some offer super service but expensive.

The following are the top brokers used by day traders around the world:

- E*Trade

- TD Ameritrade

- Tradestation

- Interactive Brokers

- Fidelity

To maintain the focus of this book, we will not review day trading brokers here. You can easily search for them online and read reviews about them.

But one of the main concerns for day traders is commission, or how much is the broker going to take with every trade you make.

Most brokers will earn from your trades whether you win or lose the trade. Therefore, savvy day traders are looking to save on trading costs as much as possible.

However, the trading cost not be your only concern. You should also balance this factor with other features of the broker that can help you become more successful like the tools you can use, research capacity, and trading platform.

So while trading cost is an important factor, it is not the only concern you need to consider.

You must also check with the current rules for day trading in your region. For example, in the United States, day traders should maintain at least $25,000 of equity in their accounts before they can trade as stipulated by the rules of the Financial Industry Regulatory Authority (FINRA).

Market Data and Trading Platform

Time is of the essence in day trading. You can be successful in your trades if you know how to execute your trades in a jiffy. You must be able to move in and out of the trades easily.

It can be a challenge to perform trades fast enough if your broker doesn't use a platform or software with hotkeys.

You need to make fast decisions so you can make extra dollars when the stock suddenly spikes. If the stock rises, you need to be able to place money in your account and make money from it fast. You certainly don't want to be bumbling with your orders. You need fast executions, which is why you really need to use a good broker as well as platform for fast order execution.

Stocks Scanner and Watch List

One of the common concerns among new traders is not knowing the stocks to trade. Every day, thousands of stocks move in the market. However, looking for a setup that is a good fit to your risk tolerance and consistent with your day trading strategy can be difficult.

You need to use a scanner to browse the market and look for good trades.

The most popular stock scanners for day traders are the following:

- StockRover
- ChartMill
- FinViz
- StockFetcher

Community of Traders

Even though day trading can be really exciting, it is also quite difficult and can be emotionally overwhelming.

It is best to join a community of retail traders and ask them questions. Consult them whenever necessary, learn new strategies, and receive some expert insights and alerts about the stock market. But don't forget that you also need to contribute in the community.

You can also talk to each other and share screens and platforms so you can watch each other as you trade. It can be a fun, interactive environment, and you can learn from each other. Through this, you can gain more knowledge and experience in day trading.

You will meet experienced traders in an online community whom you can learn much from, and you can also help other newbie traders in exploring this lucrative business.

If you join an online community, you will see that other day traders lose money often. It can make you feel good to see that losing trades is quite common in this area, and everyone, including seasoned traders still lose money in the process.

Bear in mind that you need to be an independent thinker. Basically, people may change when they join groups. They become more impulsive and unquestioning, nervously looking for a leader whose trades they can mimic. They respond with the crowd rather than using their own minds.

Online community members may be swayed by a few trends, but they could be killed if the trends suddenly reverse. Don't forget that successful traders are usually independent thinkers.

You must develop good judgment so you can decide when to trade, and when not to trade.

Chapter 5 - Introduction to Candlesticks

In order to understand the strategies explored in this book, it is important first to review price action, as well as the basic concepts of candlestick charts. In the 17th century, the Japanese started using technical analysis with the aid of early versions of candlestick charts.

The development of the candlestick analysis is credited to the Japanese rice trader named Homma. While his versions of candlestick charts and technical analysis were quite different from the modern-day version, the fundamental concepts still stand.

Candlestick charts, in their present form, first appeared in the 1850s. It is more likely that the original ideas of Homma were modified and refined over centuries of trading, and gradually developed into a charting system that day traders now use.

In creating a candlestick chart, you should have a data set, which contains the following:

1. Open price

2. Highest price in the selected time frame

3. Lowest price in the same period of number 2

4. Closing price values for each time period that you want to show

The time frame can be one minute, five minutes, one hour, one day, or any time frame that you prefer. The body refers to the hollow (white) or filled (red) portion of the candlestick.

The long thin lines below and above the body signifies the low and high range, and are referred to as wicks (also called tails or shadows). The low is marked by the bottom of the lower wick, while the high is marked by the top of the upper wick.

When the stock closes at a higher price compared to the opening, it results to a hollow candlestick. The bottom of the body represents the opening price. The top signifies the closing price.

When the stock closes lower than the opening rice, a filled candlestick is created with the top of the body signifying the opening price and the lower part of the body signifying the closing price.

In comparison to other methods of charting price action, many day traders consider candlestick charts a lot easier to interpret and more visually appealing.

Each candlestick provides an easy way to interpret price action. A day trader can easily compare the connection between the high and low as well as the open and close.

The connection between the open and close is considered vital information and forms the core of candlesticks.

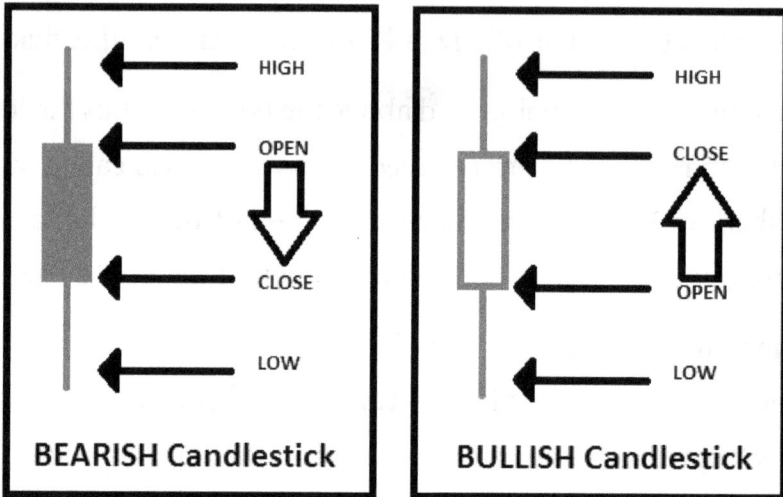

BEARISH Candlestick   BULLISH Candlestick

Here is our next rule in day trading:

Rule No. 8 - Filled candlesticks signify selling pressure, hollow candlesticks indicate buying pressure.

Traders are usually categorized into three groups:

1. Buyers

2. Sellers

3. Undecided

Sellers like to charge as much as possible and buyers want to pay as little as possible. The bid-ask spread reflects this permanent conflict. The bid refers to what a buyer offers for the merchandise.

The prices are created by the volume of traders - sellers, buyers, and undecided people. The patterns of volume and prices reflect the general behavior of the stock market.

Take note that as a day trader, your goal is to discover the balance of power between sellers and buyers, and bet on the winning group. You can see this in action if you look at candlestick charts.

Successful day traders are well-versed in social psychology and they are also trained in using computers for charting these prices. The study of mass psychology is crucial in day trading.

The presence of undecided people puts pressure on bearish and bullish trends. Sellers and buyers try to move the prices fast because they know they are surrounded by undecided traders who can easily break the deal.

Sellers know that if they try to hold out for a better price, other traders may step in and sell at lower prices. Buyers are aware that if they don't decide fast, another trader may step in and buy stocks ahead.

The group of undecided traders makes the traders more open to deal with their competitors. Sellers are selling because they are expecting prices to go down. Buyers are buying because they are expecting prices to rise.

The undecided group makes everything happen faster because they create a sense of urgency among traders. Candlesticks can signify a great deal about the general trend of the stock as well as the power of the traders in the market.

Candlesticks are initially neutral. As the time period progresses, the chart can grow to become either bullish or bearish. If a candle is born, traders don't know what it can become. They could be speculative but they don't really know what a candle is until it closes. The battle starts after a candle is born.

The bears and the bulls fight it out and the candle shows who is winning the battle. When buyers are in control, you can see the candle moving up and form a bullish candle. When sellers are in control, the candle can move down and signify a bearish market.

You are probably thinking that this is all quite obvious. However, many traders don't see candles as a battle between sellers and buyers. That little candle is a good reference that can tell you who is presently winning the battle - the sellers (bears) or the buyers (bulls). Candles with large bodies toward the upper part are bullish.

In a bullish candlestick, the buyers are in control of the price action, and there's a high chance that they will keep on pushing the price upwards. The candlestick will not only show you the price. It will also show you that the bulls are winning and that they have more power than the sellers.

Meanwhile, bearish candles signify that the sellers are in control of the price action in the market. It shows you that the sellers are presently in control, so a long position is no longer a good idea.

Candles with the filled body mean that the open was at a high and then the close was low. This indicates a bearish market.

By learning how you can read candlestick charts, you will start generating an opinion on the general behavior of the stock market. This is known as price action. Determining who is in control of the price is a very important skill in day trading. The main goal of a professional day trader is to identify the power between bears and bulls so he can win money.

If bears are stronger, you must sell and sell short. If bulls are stronger, you must buy and hold. Wise day traders stand aside if both camps are in equal power. They just allow the bears and bulls to fight with each other, and enter trades only if they are sure which side is more likely to win.

You never want to be on the wrong side of the trade. Therefore, it is important to learn how to read candlesticks and how to continuously read the price action while you are day trading.

Different Candlestick Patterns

There are numerous chart patterns that you may encounter in other day trading books. These include the following:

- Three White Soldiers

- Three Black Crows

- Stick Sandwich

- Harami

- Falling Three Methods

- Evening Star

- Morning Star

- Dragonfly

- Downside Tasuki Gap

- Dark Cloud Cover

- Abandoned Baby

- Cup and Handle

- Head and Shoulders

However, many of these chart patterns are confusing, and some of them are not useful at all. Wishful thinking is the biggest drawback of these patterns. You may find yourself detecting bearish or bullish patterns, depending on whether or not you are in the mood to trade.

So before this chapter ends, we will discuss two useful day trading patterns. Then in the next chapter, we will explore how you can trade with the aid of these patterns.

Spinning Tops

Spinning tops are candles with similarly-sized low wicks and high wicks that are typically bigger than the body and will usually be a bit more indecisive. In this pattern, the powers of sellers and buyers are almost equal.

Even though no one can control the price, the fight can continue. Normally, the volume is lower in these patterns as traders are just waiting to see who will win the fight between the buyers and the sellers.

Price trends can immediately change after the candles and they, therefore, are crucial to detect in the price action.

Doji

Doji patterns come in varying forms and shapes. However, they are all characterized by having either very small body or no body at all.

Dojis also signify indecision, which is similar to spinning tops. If you see a Doji in your chart, it means there's a strong tension happening between the bulls and the bears. Nobody has won the battle yet.

DOJI CANDLESTICKS

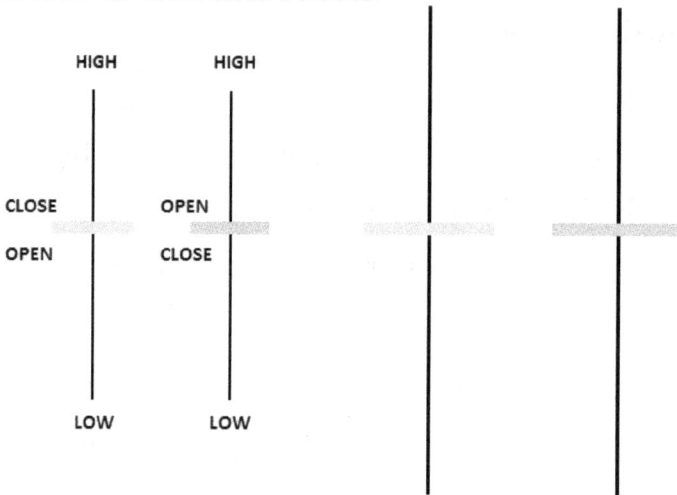

HIGH	HIGH
CLOSE	OPEN
OPEN	CLOSE
LOW	LOW

Some types of Doji such as Shooting Star are also indecision charts. However, they may show that the buyers are losing power and that the sellers are taking over.

If the bottom wick is longer like the hammer Dojis, it signifies that the sellers are not successful in trying to push the price lower. This may signify an impending takeover of price action by the bulls.

Remember, all Dojis indicate indecision and potential reversals if they are forming in a trend. When a Doji is forming a bullish trend, it signifies that the bulls have become tired, and the bears are fighting back to take over the price action.

Likewise, when a Doji forms a bearish trend, it signifies that the bears have become tired and the buyers are fighting back to take control of the price action.

After learning about these candlesticks, it is crucial that you don't get too excited, and don't depend on them too much. Always bear in mind that candlesticks are not perfect. If you take a trade each time that you see a Doji forming in a trend, you may end up with considerable losses.

Take note that these candles only signify indecision and not a specific reversal. In order to use these candles effectively, you should look for confirmation candles and use them with other forms of analysis like resistance or support levels, which we will explore in depth in the next chapter.

Chapter 6 - Effective Day Trading Strategies

Finally, we will now discuss the strategies that you can use for day trading. These strategies are based on three important fundamentals:

1. Price Action

2. Technical Indicators

3. Chart Patterns

It is essential that you understand and apply all these three elements in day trading. While some strategies only require technical indicators (like VWAP and Moving Average), it will help you a lot if you understand price action and chart patterns, so you can be a profitable day trader.

This knowledge, especially about price action comes only with regular practice. As a day trader, you must not care about the company and its revenue. You should not be distracted about the mission or vision of the company or how much money they make. Your focus must only be on the chart patterns, technical indicators, and price action.

Successful day traders also don't mix technical analysis with fundamental analysis. Day traders usually focus more on technical analysis.

As we have discussed in Chapter 4, you must look for fundamental catalysts in day stocks. The catalyst is the reason why a particular stock is running. If you have a stock that is running up to 70%, you need to determine the catalyst behind this change, and never stop until you figure that one out.

So, it's a tech company that just got patent approval or a pharmaceutical company that passed through important clinical trials. These are catalysts that can help you understand what is really going on.

Beyond this, don't bother yourself squinting over revenue papers or listening in conference calls. You should not care about these things unless you are a long-term investor.

Day traders trade fast. There are times that you may find yourself trading in time periods as short as 10 to 30 seconds, and can make thousands of dollars. If the market is moving fast, you need to make certain that you are in the right position to take advantage of the profits, and minimize your exposure to risk.

There are millions of day traders out there with different strategies. Each trader requires its own strategy and edge. You must find your spot in the market whenever you feel comfortable.

You must focus on day trading strategies because these really work for day trading. The following strategies have been proven effective in day trading. These strategies are quite basic in theory, but they can be challenging to master and requires a lot of practice.

Take note that these trading strategies give signals relatively infrequently and will allow you to participate in the markets during the ideal times just like how professional day traders do.

Also remember that in the market today, more than 60% of the volume is dominated by algorithmic trading. So you are really competing against computers. There's a big chance that you will lose against an algorithm. You may get lucky a couple of times, but supercomputers will definitely win the game.

Trading stocks against computers means that the majority of the changes in stocks that you see are basically the result of computers moving shares around. On one hand, it also means that there are certain stocks every day that will be traded on such heavy retail volume (as opposed to institutional algorithmic trading).

Every day, you have to focus on trading these specific stocks or the Apex Predators - the stocks that are usually gapping down or up on revenue.

You should hunt for stocks that have considerable interest among day traders and considerable retail volume. These are the stocks that you can buy, and together, the retail traders can still win the game against algorithmic traders.

One principle in day trading that you may find useful is that you must only choose the setups that you want to master. Using basic trading methods that are composed of minimal setups are effective in reducing the stress and confusion, and will allow you to focus more on the psychological effect of trading. This will separate the losers from the winners.

Managing Your Day Trades

Before exploring the day trading strategies in this book, it is important first to know about managing your trade. It is always intriguing when two day traders choose the same stock - the one short and the other long.

More often than not, both traders become profitable, proving that trader management and experience are more important than the stock and the strategy used by the trader.

Remember, your trade size will depend on the price of the stock and on your account and risk management. Beginners in day trading are recommended to limit the size of their shares below 1000.

For example, you can buy 800 shares, then sell half in the first target. You can bring your stop loss to break even. Then you can sell another 200 in the next target. You can keep the last

200 shares until you stop. You can always maintain some shares in case the price will keep on moving in your favor.

IMPORTANT: *Professional day traders never risk their shares all at once.*

They know how to scale into the trade, which means they buy shares at different points. They may start with 200 shares and then add to their position in different steps. For instance, for an 800-share trader, they could enter either 400/400 or 100/200/500 shares. When done properly, this is an excellent way to manage your trades and risks.

But managing the position in the system can be overly difficult. Many newbies who may attempt to do this could end up over trading and may lose their money in slippage, commissions, and averaging down the losing stocks. Rare is the chance that you may scale into a trade. Still, there are times that you can do this, especially in high-volume trades.

However, you should take note that scaling into a trade increases your risk and beginners can use it improperly as a way to average down their losing positions. We have discussed this for the sake of information, and this is not recommended for beginners.

Even though they may appear the same, there's a big difference between averaging down a losing position and scaling into a trade. For newbies, averaging down a losing position can wipe out your account, especially with small accounts that are not strong enough for averaging down.

ABCD Pattern

The ABCD Pattern is the simplest pattern you can trade, and this is an ideal choice for amateur day traders. Even though this is pretty much basic and has been used by day traders for a long time, it still works quite effectively because many day traders are still using it.

This pattern has a self-fulfilling prophecy effect, so you just follow the trend.

First sell half position after Point D Break Out

Buy between A and B

Support, Stop Loss

VOLUME!

The chart above shows an example of an ABCD pattern in the stock market. This one begins with a strong upwards move.

Buyers are quickly buying stocks as represented by point A, and making new highs in point B. In this trend, you may choose to enter the trade, but you must not be overly obsessed by the trade, because at point B, it can be quite extended and at its highest price.

Moreover, you can't ascertain the stop for this pattern. Take note that you should never enter a trade without identifying your stop. At point B, traders who purchased the stock earlier begin gradually selling it for profit and the prices will also come down.

Still, you must not enter the trade because you are not certain where the bottom of this trend will be. But if you see that the price doesn't come down from a specific level such as point C, it means that the stock has discovered possible support.

Thus, you can plan your trade and set up the, stops and a point to take the profits.

For example, OPTT (Ocean Power Technologies Inc) announced in 2016 that they closed a new $50 million deal. This one is a good example of a fundamental catalyst. OPTT stocks surged from $7.70 (Point A) to $9.40 (B) at around 9 am. Day traders who were not aware of the news waited for point B and then an indication that the stock will not go lower than a specific price (C).

If you saw that C holds support and buyers are fighting back to allow the stock price to go any lower than the price at C, you will know that the price will be higher. Buyers jumped on massively.

Remember, the ABCD Pattern is a basic day trading strategy, and many retail traders are looking for it. Near point D, the volume immediately spiked, which means that the traders are now in the trade. When the stock made a new low, it was a clear exit signal.

Here are the specific steps you can follow to use the ABCD strategy:

1. Whenever you see that a stock is surging up from point A and about to reach a new high for the day (point B), then wait to see if the price makes support higher than A. You can mark this as point C, but don't jump right into it.

2. Monitor the stock during its consolidation phase, then choose your share size and plan your stop and exit.

3. If you see that the price is holding support at point C, then you can participate in the trade closer to the price point C to anticipate the move to point D or even higher.

4. Your stop could be at C. When the price goes lower than C, you can sell. Thus, it is crucial to buy the stock closer to C to reduce the loss. (Some day traders have higher tolerance, so they wait a bit more near D to ensure that the ABCD pattern is complete. However, this is risky as it can reduce your profit).

5. When the price moves higher, you can sell half of your shares near point D, and bring your stop higher to your break-even point.

6. Sell the rest of your shares as soon as you hit your target or you feel that the price is losing momentum, or that the sellers are getting control of the price action.

Bull Flag Momentum

Bull Flag Momentum is a day trading strategy that typically works great for low float stocks, which we have discussed in Chapter 4.

Expert stock analysts consider the Bull Flag Momentum as a scalping strategy because the flags in the pattern don't usually last long. Plus, day traders should scalp the trade in order to get in quickly, make money, and then exit the market.

Below is an example of a Bull Flag pattern with one notable consolidation.

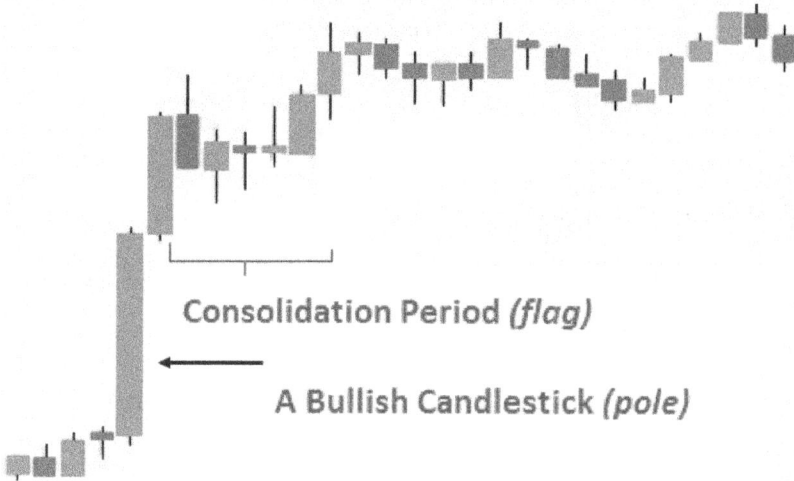

Consolidation Period *(flag)*

A Bullish Candlestick *(pole)*

This chart is called Bull Flag because it is like a flag on a pole. In this pattern, you have different large candles rising (pole) and you also have a sequence of small candles that move sideways (flag) or "consolidating" in day trading jargon.

When there is consolidation in the pattern, it signifies that traders who purchased the stocks at a cheaper price are now selling. While this is happening, the price doesn't significantly decrease because buyers are still participating in the trades, and sellers are not yet in control of the price.

Many retail traders will miss buying the stock before the Bull Flag begins. Buying stocks when the price is increasing could be risky. This is known as "chasing the stock". Successful day traders usually aim to participate in the trade during quiet periods and take their profits during wild periods.

This is the complete opposite of how newbies trade. They quickly participate or exit if the stocks start to run, but may eventually lose interest if the prices are slow-paced.

For beginners, chasing the stocks could be an account wiper. You should wait until the stock lands on a high point, then wait for consolidation. As soon as the price breaks up in the consolidation area, you can start buying stocks.

Typically, a Bull Flag will demonstrate several consolidation periods. You may enter the first and second consolidation periods. It can be risky to get into the third and fourth consolidation areas because the price has possibly been quite extended in a way that signifies that the buyers may soon lose control over the price action.

Below is an example of a Bull Flag for Rigel Pharmaceuticals (RIGL). (Next page)

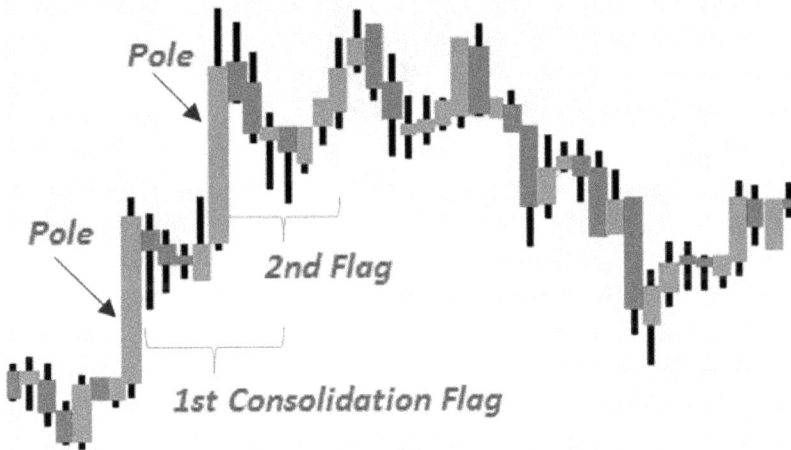

It is usually difficult to detect the first Bull Flag, and without a stock scanner, you might miss it.

As soon as you get an alert for this bull flag, you should immediately check if there's a high relative volume of trading. If yes, it becomes an ideal setup for day trading. Wait for the first consolidation period to be completed, and as soon as the stock begins to move towards its first high price for the day, you should participate in the trade.

The stop loss for the RIGL chart is the breakdown of the consolidation period. The entries and exits are marked in the picture below.

As you can see, if you have to wait for another consolidation period expecting another Bull Flag, you would probably have to be stopped. This is the reason why day traders often enter either the first or second Bull Flag, but they avoid the third one.

Here are the specific steps you can follow to use the Bull Flag Momentum strategy:

1. When you see a stock surging up, you must wait until the consolidation period is complete. Don't quickly participate in the trade or you may lose your account.

2. Watch the stock during the consolidation period. Choose your share size, as well as your stop and exit strategies.

3. Enter the trade as soon as the prices are moving beyond the highest point of the consolidation period.

Your stop loss should be at the break below the consolidation period.

4. Sell half of your shares and then take a profit on the surge. Bring your stop loss from the low of the consolidation to your break-even price.

5. Sell the rest of your shares as soon as you hit your target or you think that the price is starting to lose momentum, and the sellers are fighting back to control the price action.

Similar to the ABCD pattern, you should try to buy only around the breakeven point. The Bull Flag pattern is basically an ABCD pattern, which normally happens on low float stocks. This is fast and may vanish a lot faster. Hence, this is more or less a Momentum Scalping Strategy.

Scalpers buy stocks when they are running. They rarely like to buy during consolidation. They often drop faster and brutally, so it is crucial for you to jump only if there's a validation of the breakout.

One way to reduce your risk is to wait for the stocks to break the top of the consolidation area. Rather than buying and holding shares, scalpers usually wait for the breakout and then send their order.

Get in, scalp, and get out fast. This is the principle of momentum scalpers. Participate in the breakout, take your profit, then exit.

The Bull Flag Momentum is located inside an uptrend in a stock. It is also a long-term strategy. It is best not to short a Bull Flag and avoid trading in such momentum. It can be risky, and newbies must be cautious in trading these. If you want to test this out, try one small size at first and only after getting enough practice in simulation. You also need to quickly execute the trade through a platform designed for scalping.

Top and Bottom Reversal

Among the easiest day trading strategies are top and bottom reversals. Retail traders love them because they have specific entry and exit points, as well as a high profit to loss ratio.

In this section, we will learn the following:

- finding reversal setups with the use of stock scanners
- reading Bollinger Bands and finding extremes
- how to use Doji candlesticks to take an entry
- identifying your stops and profit targets
- trailing your winning stocks

Don't forget that what goes up must come down. So, avoid chasing extended trades. The opposite is also true. What goes down will certainly come back. If a stock begins to sell off considerably, there are two possible reasons behind:

1. Hedge funds or venture firms have begun selling their huge positions to the market and so the stock price is affected.

2. Day traders have begun short-selling the stock, but they are covering their shorts a bit sooner. This is where you must wait for an entry.

The stock will follow a reverse trend if short-sellers are trying to cover their shorts. We will illustrate this strategy using several examples so that you can precisely see what to spot on.

In the chart below, you can see the pattern of a stock that has been sold off right after the market opens.

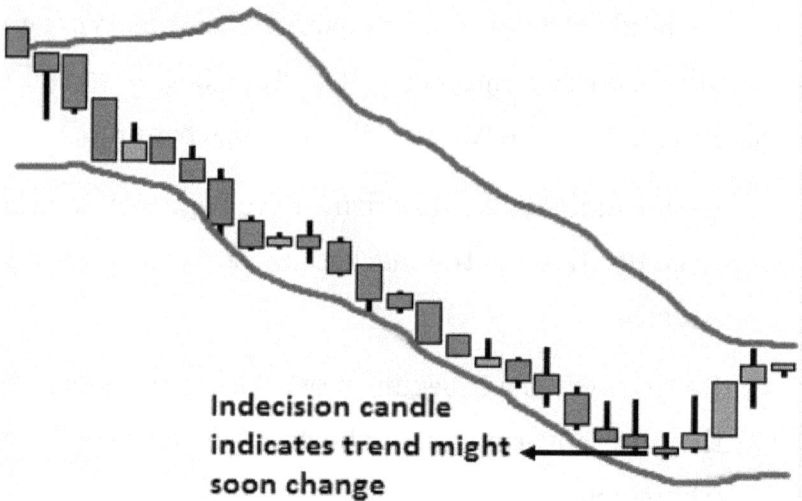

Indecision candle
indicates trend might ←
soon change

Trends like this are quite difficult to spot for the short side because if you find the spot, it might be too late to participate in the market. But always remember the day trading mantra: What goes up, will come down. Thus, you have the option to wait for a reversal.

There are four important elements in Reversal Strategy:

1. Five candlesticks moving downward or upward

2. The stock is moving outside or near the Bollinger Bands, which indicates volatility. Stocks often stay within these bands.

3. The stock will signal the extreme Relative Strength Index. Try to detect stocks with an RSI below 10 or above 90. More often than not, your day trading platform will have an RSI indicator built into the system.

The first three elements show that a stock is stretched out, and you should monitor the stock on your scanner for all this information. You should also hunt for a specific RSI level, a specific number of consecutive candles, and a specific position inside the Bollinger Bands.

4. You need to be ready if the trend is about to end, normally indicated by indecision candles like Doji or spinning top.

In reverse trading, you need to identify one of the indecision candlesticks - Dojis or spinning tops. These are indicators that the trend will soon turn into a different direction.

Remember, a Doji is a candlestick with a long wick compared to its body. Below is a picture of a bearish Doji.

Shooting Star Doji
INDECISION

Bulls in Control
buyers push
higher

Bears in Control
sellers push
lower

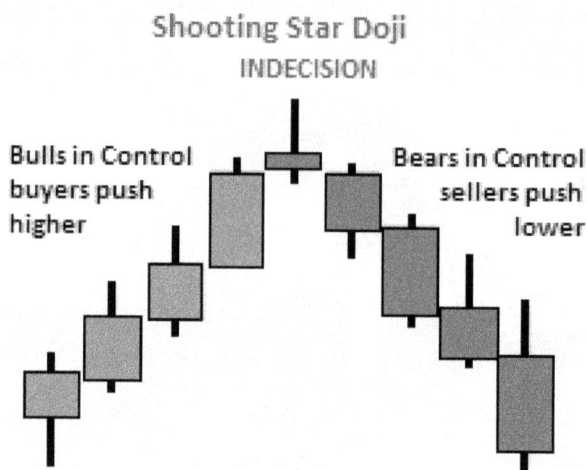

Bearish Doji has a long upper wick that some would call a top and tail, and what others would refer to as a shooting star. This candle signifies four things - the open price, the close price, the high peak of that period and the low peak of that period.

So if you have a candle with a top tail, you know that at some point during the time frame, the price moved up, wasn't able to hold at that level, and was then sold off.

It portrays a bit of a tension taking place between the sellers and the buyers in which the buyers are losing the fight. This is a good indicator that the sellers may soon control the price action and will further push down the price.

This is true with a bullish Doji, which is also depicted in the picture above. It has the longer wick below that some refer to as bottom tail or hammer. If you have a hammer candle with a bottom tail, you should know that at some point during the trading period, the price moved down, wasn't able to hold at the low levels, and was pushed up. This is an indication that there's a battle between the sellers and buyers in which the former is losing the pushdown. This signifies that the buyers are gaining control of the price and are pushing the price up.

For reversal day trading, you should look for either an indecision candlestick or Doji. These are all indications that the trend will soon change. In Reversal Strategies, you need to look for a clear validation that the pattern is starting to reverse.

What you certainly don't want is to be on the wrong side of the reversal trade. Day traders usually call this 'catching a falling blade'. It sounds bad in real life, and it sounds bad in day trading. This means that if a stock is selling off badly (the falling blade) you should not buy on the presumption that it will bounce soon.

If the stocks are on a downward trend, you need to wait for the verification of the reversal. This will normally be:

- The appearance of an indecision candle or a Doji

- The first 5-minute candle to reach a new high point

The second one is usually an entry point. You need to set your stop at the lows. For reversal day trading, the RSI must be located at the extremes (below 10 or above 90), and this final candle must be outside the Bollinger Bands.

After listing your entry requirements, you should then look for an actual entry. For most day traders, the entry is either the first minute or the first 5-minute candle to reach a new high point. The first candle that reaches the new high point is important if you've had a long run of consecutive candles making new lows.

There are instances that you need to analyze the 1-minute chart, but usually, you will need to use the 5-minute chart because this is a much better confirmation. After all, the 5-minute chart is a lot cleaner.

The first 5-minute candle to make a new high is the point at which you can get in the reversal with a stop either at the low of the day or just down around 20 to 30 cents. When a stock goes 30 to 40 cents against you, just admit the loss, acknowledge that you were mistaken about the entry and try again instead of holding.

In some instances, especially on stocks that are more volatile or expensive, you can just use a 20 or 30 cents arbitrary stop when the low of the day is quite far away. Whenever you are in one of these trades, the exit indicators are quite basic. When the stock pops up and then abruptly moves back and down on a bottom bounce, then you stop out for a loss.

When you participate in the stock and it ends up just going sideways, this is an indicator that you are probably going to see a reverse flag. This signifies that the price is probably going to continue to drop. If you get in and you hold for a while and the price stays flat, you need to exit regardless of what happens.

You might make some mistakes, but that's okay. You should not expose your account to the dangers of the unknown. You need to take the right setup, and if the setup is not yet ready, you should head to the exit.

If you make some profits, you can begin adjusting the stop, first to break-even and then to the low of the last 5-minute candle. You can then keep on adjusting your stop as you move up. You should understand that almost all of the big moves will eventually be rectified.

ALWAYS REMEMBER: *What goes up will come down.*

In reversal day trading, one of the primary benefits is the chance to monitor stocks that are moving up, while simultaneously analyzing the potential resistance points and areas that can provide a good opportunity for reversal. This will allow you to resist being impulsive and rushing into the trade.

Instead, you may take your time to monitor the trade and wait for the right moment to start the shift. Day traders usually compare reversal strategies to rubber bands. If the stock becomes really stretched, then they will eventually be due for a correction.

Hence, if a stock is really pushing down, you should understand that at some point, it will bounce and you want to be in the market when that happens. Certainly, you don't want to be in this position if you are still selling. This is a good example of catching a falling blade.

When the stocks are dropping, you need to wait for the validation of the reversal. This is often shown in the first 1-minute or the first 5-minute candlestick to make a new high point. This is your signal to enter the market and set your stop at the lows.

Bottom Reversal

The chart below for the stock history of Emergent BioSolutions (Ticker: EBS) shows a reversal.

The indecision candlestick at the end of the downtrend signifies a possible reversal, and as you will see right after that, there's a big swing back up.

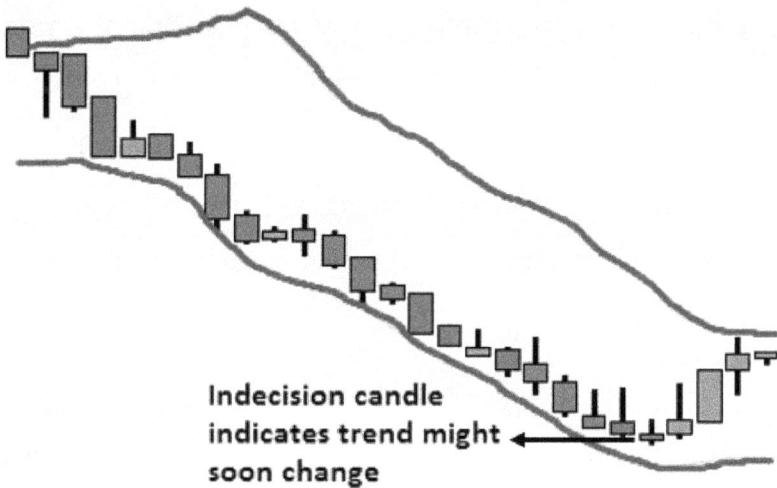

Indecision candle indicates trend might soon change

The main advantage of Reversal Trading is that it is less difficult to anticipate when stocks make significant moves. You might miss the time that the stock begins to sell off, and you don't have the time to short the stock for added revenue. However, you can always prepare for the reversal trade.

In analyzing reversals, you need to make certain that you only trade extremes. Take note that a stock that has been slowly selling off all day long usually is not suitable for a reversal.

Whenever you are working with reversals, you need to think of the stocks like rubber bands. You really need to see them stretched out to the downside or for short selling, really stretched out to the upward.

You need to see the big extension, which means you need to see the significant volume. Once you do this, you should look for several key indicators that will suggest that the tide is about to turn, and this is when you need to take the position.

Again, what goes up, will come down. More often than not, these stocks will backtrack in reverse in just a matter of minutes. It is important that you take note of the reversal time.

The key factor to become successful with the top and bottom reversals is trading the extremes. But how can you spot the extremes? Here are the things that you should look for:

1. An RSI of below 10 or above 90

2. A candlestick near or outside the Bollinger Bands

3. Five to 10 candlesticks in a series ending with a Doji or an indecision candle.

The candlesticks at the end usually show that buyers are becoming more powerful and sellers are losing their control. This often signifies the end of a trend.

But please take note that there will be instances when you will see five to 10 candlesticks in a series without much price action. The stocks might be drifting down gradually, but not fast enough for you to sense that this is an ideal reversal. You need to spot on a combination of these indicators all happening at the same time.

The high price should not be a reason to sell short. You must never argue with the decision of the crowd even if the trend doesn't make sense to you. You may choose not to follow the crowd, but never run against it.

Using all of these various factors will help you form a strategy that can be effective because of its remarkable price-loss ratio.

As a refresher, a profit-loss ratio is your average winners versus your average losers. Most newbies end up trading with dismal P/L ratio because they sell their winning stocks early and they hold their losing stocks too long.

This is an extremely common habit among new day traders. However, the Reversal Strategy lends itself to having a bigger P/L ratio.

Let's go back to the rubber band analogy. In following this strategy, you can always purchase stocks if the rubber band is stretched as far as it can. If you keep track of this right, you will be in the market as the rubber band bounces back and you can then ride the momentum right back up.

Here are the specific steps you can follow to use the Bottom Reversal Strategy:

1. Set up a scanner that can show you stocks with four or more consecutive candlesticks that will go down. Once you see a stock hitting your scanner, immediately review the volume and the resistance level or support near the stock to check if it's a good trade.

2. Wait for the confirmation of a Reversal Strategy:

   a. Formation of an indecision candlestick or bearish Doji

   b. Candles that are outside or close the Bollinger Bands

   c. RSI that is lower than 10

3. Buy the stock when you see the stock making a new 5-minute high

4. Your stop loss is the low of the previous red candlestick or the low of the day

5. Set your profit target, which could be the following:

   a. Volume Weighted Average Price (VWAP) - we will discuss this in a bit

   b. The next level of support

   c. The stock follows a new 5-minute high (buyers are once again taking control)

Top Reversal

A Top Reversal is quite similar to the Bottom Reversal. The only difference is that this strategy is ideal for short selling stocks.

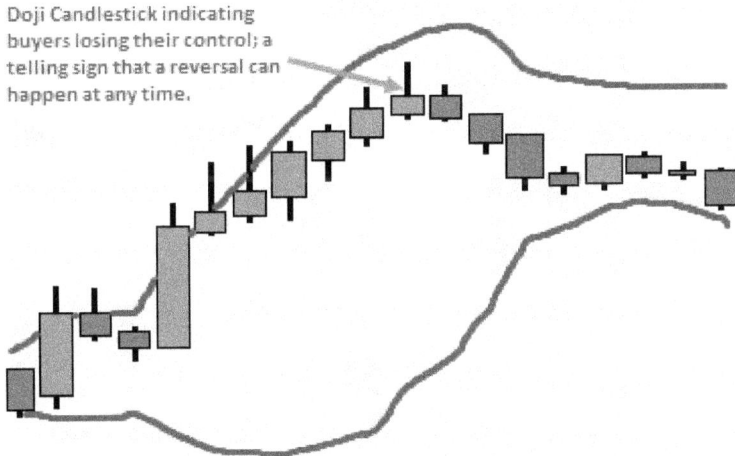

Doji Candlestick indicating buyers losing their control; a telling sign that a reversal can happen at any time.

The chart above is the stock movement of Bed Bath & Beyond Inc. Its relative volume is 21.50 and the chart shows six consecutive candles. This particular stock was trading considerably higher than its normal trend, which was caused by day traders looking for unusual trading volume.

Take note that the candles were not located near or outside Bollinger Bands. But the trade was done because it was trading with high volume and formed a good Doji above. The stock was short when the new five-minute candlestick was analyzed with the stop added as the break of the high of the last five-minute candles.

Here are the specific steps you can follow to use the Top Reversal Strategy:

1. Set up a scanner that will show you stocks with 4 or more candlesticks following a rising trend. When you see the stock hitting your scanner, immediately analyze the level of resistance or volume to check if it is a good trade.

2. Wait for the confirmation of a Reversal Strategy:

    a. Formation of an indecision candlestick or bearish Doji

    b. Candles that are outside or close to the Bollinger Bands

    c. RSI that is lower than 10

3. Buy the stock when you see the stock making a new 5-minute low

4. Your stop loss is the high of the previous candlestick or just the high of the day

5. Set your profit target, which could be the following:

    a. Volume Weighted Average Price (VWAP) - we will discuss this in a bit

b. The next level of support

c. The stock follows a new 5-minute high (buyers are once again taking control)

Some retail traders focus on reversal trades and base their whole transactions on them. Certainly, reversal trades are the most basic of the various strategies with high-risk reward ratio. Plus, it is always easy to find stocks that are ideal candidates for reversal trades.

Even experienced day traders are now into reversal trades. But take note that reversal trading is not the only effective strategy in day trading. You also need to try Support or Resistance or VWAP.

Moving Average Trend

Some day traders refer to moving averages as possible entry and exit points. Most stocks will begin a downside or upside trend respecting their moving averages in their 5-minute charts.

You can take advantage of this behavior and jump in the trend along moving average. This is below moving average for short selling or above the moving average for going long.

Most newbies usually wonder why moving averages are becoming resistance or support. The main reason is that many traders are looking at these lines and they are making decisions based on these averages. Hence, they have a self-fulfilling prophecy effect. There's no basic reason behind moving averages being resistance or support line.

Many day traders are using 50 and 200 simple moving averages (SMA) and 9 and 20 exponential moving averages (EMA).

The SMA refers to the moving average that is calculated by adding the nearest closing prices, then dividing this number by the time period in the average computation. Short-term moving averages quickly respond to changes in the price of the underlying price. On the other hand, long-term averages require time to react.

EMA is a moving average that highlights the recent price data of the SMA. It responds faster to recent price movements than SMA. The formula for computing the EMA simply includes the SMA and a multiplier.

Most charting software for day trading have built-in moving averages. These are usually ready to use and you don't need to adjust the settings.

Below is an example chart that shows an EMA of nine:

As you should have noticed by now, the stock has formed a Bull Flag and a consolidation period on EMA 9. If you see this signal, it means there's a support holding, so you should enter the market and ride the trend until the price breaks the moving average.

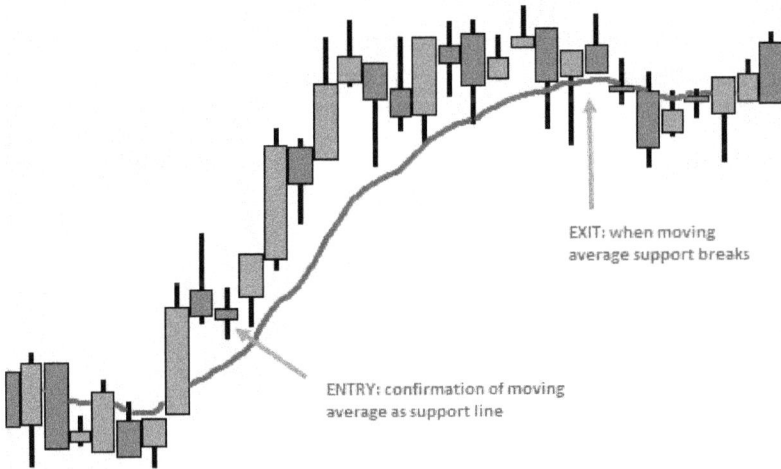

EXIT: when moving average support breaks

ENTRY: confirmation of moving average as support line

Here are the specific steps you can follow to use the Moving Average Strategy:

1. Keep track of the stock if you notice a trend is forming on its moving averages.

2. Immediately look at the trading data of the previous day to check if the stock is responding to the moving averages in a 5-minute chart. You may follow the 50 and 200 SMA and 9 and 20 EMA used by many day traders.

3. Once you learn which moving average is more suitable to the behavior of the trade, buy the stock after

confirming the moving averages as a support. Ideally, you should buy as close as possible to the moving average line. Try to set your stop at 5 cents below the break of the moving average.

4. Ride the trend until the break of the moving average.

5. Avoid using trailing stops, and always monitor the trend with your own eyes. Don't rely on algorithm for this strategy.

6. Take your profit if you see that the stock is moving really high away from the moving average. Don't wait until the break of moving average for your exit.

Some day traders avoid trading moving averages. They see them as potential levels of resistance or support, but they rarely make any trend based on moving averages trend. Take note that in a trend trade strategy, you are often exposed in the market for a significant period.

Some trends may last for as long as three hours, and this could be too exhausting for some day traders. Another drawback with moving average trading is that you are not certain in the stock you want to trade. It can be difficult to know which moving average is accurately acting at a resistance or support level.

As we have discussed, your day trading strategy should depend on your personality, risk tolerance, account size, and trading psychology. This is on top of the brokers and tools that you are using.

Take note that day trading strategies are not something that you can mimic just from attending a class, speaking with a day trader or reading a book. You need to carefully develop your preferred approach, and then stick with it. It makes no sense to stick to moving averages if the ABCD pattern helps you to become profitable.

Volume Weighted Average Price (VWAP)

As you practice day trading, you need to slowly create your own method and stick with it. The best day trading strategy is the one that works for you. There's no good or bad in any of these strategies. It really is a matter of personal preference.

The day trading strategies we have discussed so far were the fundamentals. Over time, numerous strategies have been developed by day traders as they see fit for their choices. One example is the Volume Weighted Ave. Price (VWAP).

A trading benchmark, VWAP is used by retail traders to provide the average price a stock has traded at for the day. This metric is based on the stock price and volume. It is crucial because it will provide you with insight into both the value and the trend of a particular stock.

While other moving averages are computed based only on the stock price in the chart, VWAP also considers the number of the shares that the stock is traded on each price. Most day trading platforms have a built-in VWAP indicator, and you can use this without changing your default settings. This metric will help you quickly identify who is in control of the price action - sellers or buyers.

If the stock is trading above VWAP, it signifies that the buyers are in general control of the price action. If the stock is trading below the VWAP, it is a safe assumption that the sellers are in general control of the price. VWAP trading can be a walk in the park for day trading beginners because so many traders are looking at this metric and are making their decisions in reference to it.

Thus, newbies can easily be on the right side of the trade. If the stock is trying to break the VWAP but not able to, you can instead short the stock because there's a high chance that other traders are also watching the trade, and will also start to short.

A VWAP trading strategy is a simple and easy strategy that you can follow. Many day traders often short stocks if the retail crowd is trying to break the VWAP, but are clearly failing.

Below is an example chart where a VWAP strategy is used:

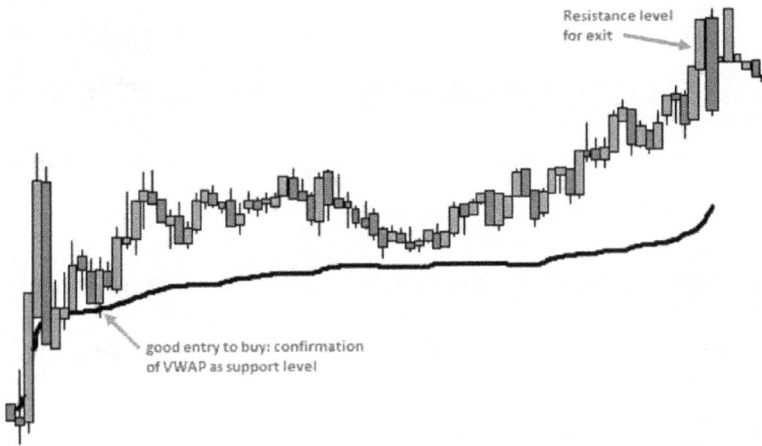

The day trader noticed that this stock rallied support over VWAP, so he bought 1000 shares with the projection that this will move toward an increase. His stop was close under VWAP. He first sold half of his shares and then moved his stop to break-even.

Here are the specific steps you can follow to use the VWAP strategy:

1. Whenever you make your watch list for your day trading, keep track of the price action around VWAP.

2. If a stock is moving towards VWAP, then wait until validation of the VWAP will support or break.

3. You may choose to buy as close as possible to reduce the risk. Your stop will be a break and close the 5-minute chart under VWAP.

4. Keep the trade until you hit your revenue target or until you reach a new resistance or support level.

5. Sell half of your shares near your target profit or resistance or support level

6. Move your stop to your entry point or break-even.

A similar method can also work if you want to short a stock.

Resistance or Support Trading

Horizontal resistance or support trading is another popular approach in day trading. Remember this: the stock market doesn't know diagonal trends. It only recognizes price levels.

This is why horizontal resistance or support lines are ideal benchmarks. On the other hand, diagonal trend lines can be subjective and can often lead to false assumptions.

As a matter of fact, trend lines are among the most deceptive of all day trading tools. You can easily draw a trend line across zones or prices in a manner that can affect its slope and its meaning. For example, if you are predetermined to buy, you may have the tendency to draw a steeper trend line.

Support is a price level where buyers are powerful enough to disrupt or reverse a downtrend. Once a downtrend hits support, it may bounce like a diver who hits the bottom of the sea, and then quickly pushes away. Horizontal lines represent support on a chart as you will see in the figure below.

On the other hand, resistance is a price level where sellers are powerful enough to disrupt or reverse an uptrend. If an uptrend hits resistance, it behaves like a person who hits a branch while climbing a mountain. It will stop and might even fall. Horizontal lines that connect two or more stops represent resistance on the charts.

Minor resistance or support may cause the trends to pause. Meanwhile, major resistance or support may cause the trends to reverse.

Traders sell at resistance and buy at support, which makes their effect a self-fulfilling prophecy. Using this approach, you can shortlist the stocks that you are interested to trade based on the criteria we have established in Chapter 4.

As a reminder, you need to choose stocks with significant catalysts such as news, high revenue report, or new approval from regulatory authorities. These stocks are the ones that day traders are monitoring and planning to trade.

Before the market opens, you can return to your daily charts and find price levels that were recorded in the past to be critical. Looking for price resistance or support levels can be tricky and requires a lot of experience in day trading.

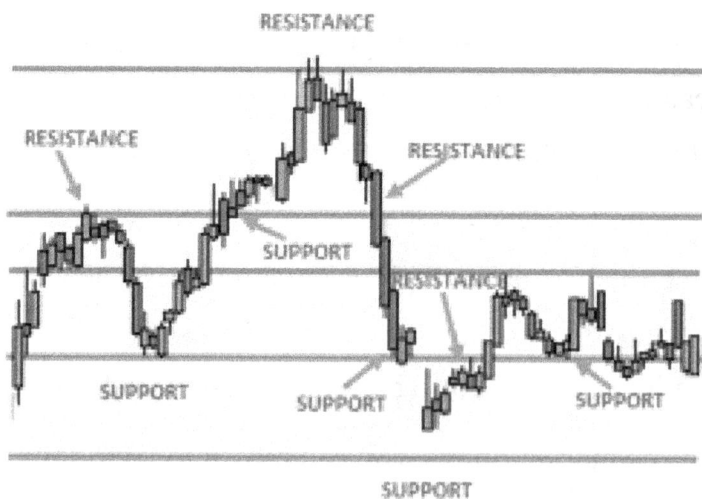

The chart on the left shows the daily chart of SCTY stock without the resistance or support lines. The image on the right includes these lines.

Resistance or support lines in daily charts are not always easy to find. In some instances, you will not be able to draw anything clear. If you can't see anything clear, then you don't have to draw anything.

There's a good chance that other traders will also not see these lines clearly and so there's no point in forcing yourself to draw resistance or support lines. In this case, you can plan your trades based on Moving Averages or VWAP that we have discussed earlier.

Tips in Drawing Resistance or Support Lines

1. You may see Doji or indecision candlesticks in the area of resistance or support because this is where traders are closely battling each other.

2. Whole dollars and half-dollars often act at resistance or support level. If you can't find a resistance or support line around these figures on a daily chart, take note that on daily charts, these figures may behave like an invisible resistance or support line.

3. You must always look at the previous data before you draw the lines.

4. Lines that are touching the price lines have more value. Emphasize these lines.

5. Only the resistance or support lines in the present price range are essential. If the stock price is presently at $40, it makes no sense to find resistance or support lines in the area when it was $80. There's a low chance that the stock will move and reach this region. Look only at the resistance or support area that is close to your day trading range.

6. Resistance or support lines are regions, and not exact figures. For instance, if you find an area around $38.16 as a support line, you should expect the price action movement around this figure, but not precisely $38.16. Depending on the stock price, an area of 10 to 20 cents is a safe assumption. The actual support line might be anything from $38.36 to $38.45

7. The price should have a clear bounce form its level. If you are not sure if the price has bounced in its level, then it is possibly not a resistance or support level.

8. In day trading, it is recommended to draw resistance or support lines across the extreme prices instead of areas where the bulk of the bars has stopped. This is the total opposite of swing trading. In swing trading, you have to draw resistance or support lines across the edges of the congestion areas where the bulk of the bars halted instead of the extreme prices.

Drawing resistance or support lines, while tricky, can be really simple once you have done it a lot of times.

Here are the specific steps you can follow to use the VWAP strategy:

1. When you create your watch list for the day, immediately look at the daily charts for the watch list and look at the area of resistance or support.

2. Keep track of the price action around these areas on a 5-minute chart. If an indecision candle forms around this region, this is a confirmation of that level, and you can enter the trade.

3. Minimize your risk by buying in as close as possible. Stop at the break and close the 5-minute chart below the resistance or support level.

4. Take your profit near the next resistance or support level.

5. Keep the trade open until you hit your target profit or you reach a new resistance or support level.

6. Sell half of your shares near the profit target or resistance/support level, and move your stop near your entry point or for break-even.

7. Consider closing your trade if there are no clear resistance or support levels.

You can also use the same approach if you short a stock.

Other Day Trading Strategies

Day traders usually choose their strategies according to specific factors like size of the account, amount of time that you can commit to trading, risk tolerance, personality, and trading experience.

Ideally, you should develop your own trading strategy and personalize it to your own preferences. Your psychology and risk tolerance are most likely different from other day traders, and from those other traders.

You are probably not comfortable with a $1000 loss, but traders who have big accounts can easily tolerate the loss and eventually make a profit out of the trade.

You can't just mimic other day traders. You should develop your own risk management plan and strategy. Some retail traders largely focus on technical indicators such as moving average crossover, moving average convergence divergence (MACD), or RSI.

There is a lot of technical indicators out there. Some day traders believe they hold the secret and it could be a mix of moving average crossover or RSI. But these are not always effective in the long run.

Basically, you can't participate in a trade using a systemic method and then allow indicators to guide your entry and exit points. This is the core of our next rule:

Rule No. 9 - Technical indicators will only guide you.

They should not dictate you.

Algorithmic programs are trading all the time. If you set up a system for trading that has no input or requires no human insight, then you are in the realm of algorithmic trading. This is not ideal for day traders as you will eventually lose against investment firms that have well-funded algorithms and sizeable trading capital.

Certainly, we can use the RSI in your scanner to guide your day trading strategy, especially for reversal trading. There are also scanners that depend on high or low RSI, but these are more conditioned to look for stocks. By any means, these are not buy/sell indicators.

Develop Your Own Day Trading Strategy

While you should understand these day trading strategies, you should try to find your own place in the market. You could be a 5-minute trader or a 1-hour trader. Some are even swing traders who are more comfortable working with daily or weekly charts.

The stock market is huge, and you can find your own place. You need to consider the lessons in this book as puzzle pieces that together make up the bigger picture of day trading. You can pick up some of the pieces in this book, and you can also choose some of the pieces from your own research. Eventually, you can have all the pieces you need to create your own unique trading strategy that really works for you.

Don't expect that everything you have learned here is applicable to you. You can follow some of the strategies here or completely ditch other strategies you find not useful. The important thing that you need to do for now is to create your own strategy based on your risk tolerance, account size, and personality.

There is a lot of day trading strategies that you have learned here and there will be a lot more, which you will encounter as you practice this trade. As a newbie, you should try to master one strategy. Once you have tested the water with one strategy, you can become a professional trader who has made some profit in the trade. The more you practice, the more you will learn.

This is a career where you must survive until you can make it. You can begin casting out a bit, but first, you have to master just one strategy. You may choose Reversal Strategy, a Bull Flag Momentum Strategy, VWAP trade, or you can develop your own. Limit your options, create your area of strength into a doable approach, and then use this strategy to survive until you are more knowledgeable and experienced enough to create other unique strategies. Never trade without a plan.

Always plan your trade and trade according to your plan. You can't just change your plan once you jump in the trade and you are in an open position.

The reality in day trading is that the profits are not guaranteed. You will lose money. The majority of day traders today are not aware of the insights that you have learned from this book. Many of them are using day trading strategies that are not even proven effective. Some of them don't even have a strategy in place. They follow a bit of advice from someone, or they mimic someone they know.

That method is dangerous. You can quickly lose your trade, and then you may wonder what happened. You may choose to practice for weeks in a day trading simulator, and then trade a bit with real cash for one week, then return to the simulator to improve your weak areas or practice new strategies for another two weeks. This approach is fine.

Even seasoned day traders are still using simulators when they want to test out a strategy that they are working on. While learning the insights in this book and practicing in simulators, your focus should be to develop a strategy to guide your live trades.

There's no mad rush in this career. Day trading is a marathon, and not a sprint. This is not about making $20,00 in one day (even though it is not impossible to do that in day trading). This is about honing a set of skills that you can use to become successful in this career.

Chapter 7 - Day Trading Process

One underlying principle in day trading that you can follow as a beginner is mastering only a few setups that are solid yet profitable. As a matter of fact, following simple trading strategies composed of several minimal setups can help in minimizing stress and confusion. It will also allow you to focus more on the psychological elements of day trading.

After learning the fundamentals of day trading strategies, let's go over the actual process for planning and making a trade. At this point, you should have a basic understanding of the setup that you want to trade. However, as a newbie, you may find it difficult to plan and initiate your trade beforehand.

Setting up your trade can be easy. The challenge starts in figuring out when to enter or exit a trade. This is where you can really make money or break your account.

The key to prevent losses in day trading is to develop a process. Remember, you must plan your trade and trade your plan. Seasoned day traders usually follow a systematic approach to day trading.

Successful day traders know what to do every day. They have a morning routine, they know what to do in developing their watch list, they organize their trade plan, they initiate their trade based on their plan, they execute the trade based on their plan, and at the end of the day, they assess what happened.

You should bear in mind that what makes a trade lucrative is the proper execution of all the steps in the process described above. Write down your reasons for exiting and entering each trade. Anyone can buy a book on day trading and read every page. However, only a small percentage has the discipline for proper execution.

Even if you have a good setup, you can still lose money if you choose the wrong stocks to trade. These include stocks that are manipulated by institutional traders or computers. Or even if you find proper stocks to trade, you could have jumped in at the wrong time. A wrong timing could mess up your trade plan and you will eventually lose money. You can look for good stocks to trade, then enter the trade properly. But if you don't get out at the right time, you may transform a winning trade into a losing one.

All the steps in the day trading process are crucial. Consider something significant that you always do in your life, and then think about how you can do it efficiently. Now, think about how you do it at the present. This is a remarkable thought process for day traders. If you take a trade, you need to make certain that you are focused on the right things either before you enter the trade and during the trade.

Developing a thought process can take away most of the emotional hang-ups that day traders experience when they are looking to jump in a trade, and also managing the trade when they are inside the market.

This brings us to the tenth and final rule in day trading:

Rule No. 10 - Don't allow your emotions to cloud your judgment.

It can be difficult for you to make money in day trading if you are too emotional. If you allow your emotions to rule your decisions, you will lose a lot of money.

Knowledge and regular practice can provide you with a perspective of what really matters in day trading, your approach in day trading, and how you can improve your skills.

Once you have a perspective on what is important, you can easily identify the particular processes that you should concentrate on. The key here is to precisely know your approach.

Beginners usually learn their lessons the hard way - they lose money. But you will realize that trading, following your plan, and the discipline that is inherent in your trading approach can be a reflection of your daily habits, which can contribute a lot to becoming a successful day trader.

For example, Ben is a day trader who has been in the equities and forex market for nearly eight years. Whenever he starts his trading process, he follows the same routine when he gets up in the morning.

He always works out in the morning before the trading session begins. He wakes up at 6 am every day, then he hits the gym from 6:00 am to 7 am. He comes home, takes a shower, and then at 7:30 am he begins writing his trading plan for the day.

Ben discovered that when his body has not been active before trading, he makes poor decisions. There are actually clinical studies correlating exercise to decision making. Individuals who regularly exercise have outstanding scores on performance tests and neuropsychological exams. They also have higher scores on tests that measure memory, cognitive flexibility, and information processing.

Your brain is your number one tool in day trading, so make sure that you take care of it. In financial markets, just being better than average is not enough. You should be excellent in order to win every day.

Sadly, day trading usually attracts people with strong impulses such as gamblers and other people who feel that they are entitled to win. Avoid these mindsets. Stop behaving like an irresponsible teenager.

You must begin developing the discipline of a master. Masters think, feel, and act differently than average people. Try to look within yourself and eliminate your illusions. Change your old methods of acting, thinking, and being.

It can be extremely difficult to change, but if you really want to be a profitable day trader, you need to work on changing and improving yourself. In order to succeed, you need the right form of motivation, know-how, and discipline.

Day trading is a serious business. If you treat this as a hobby, you will not go far.

Successful day traders follow specific morning routines. They wake up early in the morning, they are engaged in exercise, they eat healthy meals, and they are disciplined. As a result, they are awake, alert, and motivated to win the trade.

Following a morning routine can significantly help you prepare your mind for day trading. So regardless of what you do, starting your day in the same routine can lead to sizeable profits.

Rolling out of your bed and then haphazardly opening your computer will not prepare you for the stock market. Sitting on your couch in your pajamas is not the right position to win the game.

Ben's watch list comes from a particular scan that he uses every day. He doesn't need to look from other sources because he is confident that the stocks appearing on his scanner are set up for the trade he wants. He analyzes every stock, in the same manner, using his checklist where he can figure out if it is actually a good trade. His watch list is completed by 8:00 am, and he will not add anything to this list because there is no time to analyze new stocks and plan another trade.

When the market opens at 9:30 am, Ben has his plans in place written on his notebook. He has a good memory but he still writes his plan.

> *What will I do if the stocks set up to the long side?*
>
> *What will I do if the stocks set up to the short side?*
>
> *What kind of setups do I wish to see?*
>
> *What is my profit target for the day?*
>
> *Where should I place my stops?*
>
> *Is the profit area big enough for the trade to be good?*

By asking these questions, Ben has a clear advantage over other day traders because he has a battle plan, and all he needs to do is to stick with it. If he has his plan written down on a piece of paper, he can easily review it. This eliminates the anxiety that he used to feel whenever the market opens.

When the market opens, Ben will start looking for his signals and triggers to jump in the trade. There are instances when Ben second guesses himself, but those are rare instances. He has his targets written out, including the technical indicators that he uses for placing his stops. After entering the market, he just needs to focus on hitting his targets and cashing in his profits.

Some day traders believe that knowing the time to get out is the most difficult part of day trading. It can be really hard not to get out of the trade too early, especially if you don't have a plan.

When you have a trading plan and you follow it, you are in a better position to win the trade and cut your losses fast rather than the other way around. This can also help you in keeping your emotions in check during the trade.

It can also help you a lot if you know how to filter out the noise. This will allow you to focus on the trade instead of overanalyzing the situation. After you are done trading, you can start reflecting on how well your plan worked, and how much profit you earned by following your plan. You can start reflecting your trades at night when you review and recap your trades of the day.

Reflection is an important part of the day trading process. Just because you have made money during the day doesn't mean you are a successful day trader. Assessing how you play both sides of the trade is extremely important.

You can start your own trading journal if you want or watch the recap in your trading platform. You can save these insights later for your reference. Some lessons are harder than others because they include losses. However, you should be confident that in due time, you will improve your skills.

Following a process in day trading is crucial because it will help you prepare for trading and provide you the focus for proper execution. It can also help you filter out the emotional and crowd noise. It will provide you with a higher chance of success and offer you a tool to review and assess your trades.

If you know how to focus on the right processes, in the right manner, then you can develop your own approach to successful day trading.

Chapter 8 - Forex Day Trading

At this point, you should have sufficient information about day trading. We also have given you examples, but they are all about equities.

Day trading is not only limited to the equities or stock market. You can also use day trading strategies for other instruments such as foreign exchange, options, and futures markets.

Forex Day Trading

The foreign exchange market (simply known as forex) refers to the actual market where market participants can trade or speculate currencies. It plays an important role in the global economy because the currencies must be converted first before anyone can facilitate business.

For example, if you are located in Japan and you like to buy 300 sacks of curry powder from India, you need to pay your supplier in Rupees (INR). But before you can do that, you need to exchange the corresponding value of Japanese Yen (JPY) into INR.

Forex is also vital in tourism. A Chinese tourist cannot pay in Yuan when in Paris because Yuan is not the accepted currency in the country. Hence, he must exchange Yuan to Francs at the current price.

The need to exchange currencies for either business or personal transactions affect the high liquidity and volatility in the forex market. In fact, the forex market is a lot bigger than the equities market. It is estimated that around $5 Trillion are traded in the forex market every day.

An important feature of this global trading platform is that there's no particular organization or group that manages the trade. You may trade in the forex market via digital channels through over the counter (OTC) transactions.

Instead of a central platform, forex transactions can happen online in several regions around the globe. Unlike in the equities market where you need to wait for the market to open, you can trade in the forex market 24 hours a day and 5 days a week, because the currencies are traded in different financial spots such as Paris, Hong Kong, Zurich, New York, Sydney, Singapore, Frankfurt, Tokyo, London, and New York. This passes through various time zones, so if the trade is closing in Singapore, the platform is just starting in London.

There are three general options in forex market trading:

    1. Spot Market

2. Futures Market

3. Forwards Market

Spot market trading is considered as the busiest financial market today because it serves as the main platform for the futures and forwards market. In the past, the futures market has the highest level of activity as it used to cater to private investors, as well as day traders.

However, with the emergence of online forex trading, the spot market has experienced a considerable flow of investment and is now competing with the futures market as one of the busiest trading platforms for speculators and day traders.

Day traders are often trading in the spot market. The forwards market and the futures market are often reserved for organizations that need to hedge their risks to a particular date in the future.

Forex Spot Market

The forex spot market is the platform where day traders can buy and sell currencies based on the prevailing rates. The price can be affected by the current demand and supply and is also affected by different factors such as political situations, economic performances, current interest rates, and currency pair performance perception.

In the spot market, the spot deal refers to the final deal. This is a two-channel transaction wherein one party will provide an agreed currency rate. The transaction is completed if the position is closed.

While the spot market is known as the platform where day traders can trade in present commodities, the trades can be settled also in a matter of days or weeks. In that case, it is known as swing trading and not day trading.

Forex Futures and Forwards Markets

While the spot market is known as the platform where day traders can trade in present commodities, the trades can be settled also in a matter of days or weeks. In that case, it is known as swing trading and not day trading.

On the other hand, there's no actual trading of currencies in the futures and forwards markets. Rather, market participants deal with contracts, which signify a claim to a particular form of currency and a particular unit price. The trade is only settled at a future date.

In the futures market, the trades are settled based on a standard size and the settlement date for public financial markets such as Chicago's Mercantile Exchange. The futures market in the US is administered by the National Futures Association. The contracts in the futures market have specific details including the units for trading, settlement date, and the increase in price.

In the forwards market, the contracts are exchanged over the counter between two traders who will agree on specific terms. Global companies are primarily trading agreements in the forwards market to hedge against the fluctuations in the exchange market. Therefore, this platform is usually not ideal for day traders.

Bear in mind that an important differentiating factor between the forex markets is how we quote currencies. Within the forwards or futures markets, the currencies are always quoted against the US dollar.

Therefore, the pricing is conducted in terms of how many USD you need to purchase a single unit of a certain currency. Take note that in the forex spot market, some currencies are quoted against the US dollars, while there are also quotes where USD is quoted against them. Hence, the quotes from the futures / forwards market and the spot market will not usually become aligned with each other.

As an example, in the forex spot market, the Euro is quoted with the US dollars as EUR/USD. This is also the manner used for quoting currencies in the futures and forwards market. Hence, if the Euro becomes stronger than the US dollar in the spot market, there is also a high tendency for the currency to rise in the futures and forwards markets.

Meanwhile, in the case of the USD / JPY currency pair, USD is quoted against JPY. The current quote in the spot market for this fx pair is 110.27, which means that $1 will buy 110.27 Japanese yen. But in the futures fx market, the quote will be .0090 or (1/110.27), which means that 1 Japanese yen will buy .0090 US dollars.

Therefore, a slight increase in the USD/JPY in the spot market will result in a fall in the yen futures rate since USD will be stronger against the yen, and so one unit of yen will buy fewer dollars.

Forex Swing Trading

This medium-term forex trading strategy is typically used over a period of days to weeks. Swing traders will usually look to set up trades on swings to lows and highs over a certain period of time.

Its purpose is to filter out the erratic movements in the price, which is common in intraday trading. This is also used to prevent setting narrowly placed stop losses, which can force the traders to stop a trade for a short-term market flow.

It is true that the forex market is filled with ratios, charts, and numbers. However, this game is more of an art than science. Similar to artistic endeavors, talent is a strong foundation, but it will only get you so far with your effort and improvement.

Successful traders develop their skills through discipline and practice. They perform self-evaluation to see what is driving their trades, and learn how they can keep greed and fear out of the equation. In this section, we will discuss the tips and tricks that a beginner can use to become successful in forex trading.

Establish your goals and select a trading style that is compatible with your personality

Before beginning a single trade in the forex market, it is crucial that you have some concept of where you want to go and how you can work every day to achieve this destination.

Also, it is crucial that your goals in mind are clear as to what you want to achieve. You should also be certain that the trading strategy you choose will help you achieve your goals.

Take note that every type of trading strategy requires a specific approach and every style is suitable to different risk profiles. For instance, day trading can be ideal for you if you are not comfortable with an open position in the market.

Meanwhile, if you have capital that you believe will take advantage of the appreciation of a trade over a period of several months, then position trading might be ideal for you. Just make certain that your personality is suitable for the trading style you do.

Select a trading methodology and be consistent

Before you start any trade, you should have enough knowledge about the forex market so you can execute your trades with confidence. You should know the specific information you need so you can make the best decision about whether to exit or enter a trade.

Some traders are using technical analysis, while others prefer to look at the underlying fundamentals of the economy of the company, and then use charts to find out the best time to enter the trade. Take note that market fundamentals can drive the long-term trend.

Chart patterns, on the other hand, may provide you with short-term trading opportunities. Just be consistent regardless of the methodology you prefer, and make certain to be flexible as well. The methodology must catch up with the changing forex market platform.

Carefully select your entry and exit frames

Most beginners in forex trading experience confusion because of the opposing data that they may encounter in evaluating charts in various time frames.

For example, the information that can be extracted from an intraday chart could indicate a sell signal, which may show up as a buying signal when viewed in a weekly chart. Hence, if you depend on an intraday chart and use a weekly chart to look for the best time entry, make certain that the two charts are in sync. When the weekly chart indicates a buying signal, you should also wait until the daily chart also shows a buying signal.

Work on the trade expectancy

It is crucial to make sure that whichever system you use, it should be reliable. You can do this by calculating the expectancy.

Using a specific formula, you can revisit past trends and gauge all the trades that you won against the trades that you lost. Then, you can figure out the profitability of the winning trades against how much you have lost on losing trades.

Check your previous 10 trades, then figure out if you have made a profit or loss. Write the trades down and get the total of all the trades you won then divide the answer by the no of trades you won. Below is the formula. W refers to the average winning trade, L refers to the average losing trade, while P refers to the percentage of winning ratio.

$$E= [1+ (W/L)] \times P - 1$$

For example, in your previous 10 trades, you won seven trades, and three losses, 70 percent is your win ratio. If the seven trades gained $3,000, then the average win is $3000/7 = $428.57.

If your total loss was $ 1,000, then your average loss is $1,000/3 = $ 333.33. In using the formula above, you will get: E=[1+ (428.57/333.33)] x 0.7 -1 = 0.60 or 60%, which means 60 percent reliability of the system that can provide you 60 cents on a dollar in the long run.

Create positive feedback loops

You can create a positive feedback loop if your trades are implemented according to your strategic plan. A positive feedback pattern can be created if you execute a trade based on your plan.

Success can breed success, which could in turn provide the confidence you need, especially if the trade is profitable. The habit of sticking to your plan, despite some losses that you may encounter in the process can still result in a positive feedback loop.

Concentrate on your trading strategy and don't be afraid of small losses

In playing the forex market, you should take note that there is a risk of losing all your money. Hence, you should only use your excess money and not gamble your money for necessities such as college fund.

Successful traders consider their trading fund as a game fund.

When the game is over, the money is all spent. This attitude can help you to be more positive while trading in forex. Psychologically, you can be well-prepared to accept even small losses.

This is crucial in how you can handle risks successfully. You can become a successful forex trader if you concentrate on your trades and you learn from your minor losses.

Setting Up Your Forex Day Trading Account

Forex day trading is quite similar to stock market day trading because you have first to open your own trading account. Similar to the stock market, every forex account, as well as the services you can take advantage of can be different. Hence, it is crucial that you look for the most suitable platform for you.

In this section, we will discuss the important factors that you should consider when choosing a foreign exchange account.

Trading Leverage

When we speak of leverage, we refer to the opportunity to take control of bigger amounts of cash with minimal capital from your own pocket. The leverage level is directly proportional to the risk level.

Take note that the leverage amount on a platform could vary, according to the features of the account on its own. However, the most popular one is 50:1 leverage. Some accounts could offer a maximum leverage of 250:1.

For example, the maximum leverage of 100:1 signifies that for each dollar that you hold in the brokerage account, you can use up to $100. For instance, if you have an account balance of $100, the brokerage can allow you to trade as much as $10,000 in the fx market.

This leverage could also define the total amount that you can hold in your account or your margin for trading a specific amount. In the stock market, the margin is often at 50%, and the leverage could be 50:1, which can be at least 2%.

In general, leverage is regarded as a primary advantage of trading in the foreign exchange market, because this will allow you to create substantial gains with minimal capital. But leverage could also have extreme downsides when a trade is moving in the opposite direction because the losses could also be big.

With this leverage type, there is always the actual probability that your losses are higher than what you have invested, even though most accounts have safeguard stops to prevent the account from hitting negative. As such, it is crucial that you take note of this when you open a brokerage account, and once you identify your preferred leverage, you can understand the involved risks more.

Fees and Commissions

Another major advantage of forex platforms is that investing through them could be done through commissions, which is unlike stock market accounts where you need to pay a broker a certain fee for every trade.

You are now directly dealing with market players, and you don't have to pass through another layer such as brokers.

Every time you enter a trade, it is the market makers, which can seize the spread. Hence, when the ask/bid for a forex market is 1.5300/50, the market maker can capture the difference between the points.

In setting up your own forex account, be sure to take note that every firm has various spreads on currency pairs that you trade. Even though they are usually different by only several pips, this could be substantial when you are planning to do a lot of trading.

Hence, in setting up an account, be certain that you are aware of the pip and spread of specific currency pairs that you are interested in trading.

You must take note that there are several differences between every forex platform and the programs or software that they are offering. Hence, it is crucial to review every firm before you make a commitment. Every forex trading company may offer various levels of programs and services including the fees beyond and above the actual costs of trading.

Moreover, because of the less strict conditions in the foreign exchange market, you should find a reliable firm. When you are also not completely confident to trade with real cash, you can also try trading in practice accounts or demos.

How to Start Day Trading in the Forex Market

After understanding the most crucial factors in opening your own forex account, it is time to look into what specifically you could trade within the platform. The two primary methods in trading in the forex market include the actual trading (selling and buying) of forex pairs, in which you short currency and long another.

Another method is via buying the derivatives that monitor the fluctuations of a particular currency pair. These strategies are quite similar to the common techniques used in the stock market.

Basically, buying and selling the currency pair is the most popular method, much in a similar manner that many traders are buying and selling currency units.

In this setting, a trader may hope that the currency pair's value will change in a profitable way. If you choose to short a pair, it signifies that you are betting on the possibility that the pair's value will fall.

For instance, let's assume that you want a short position for the USD/JPY pair. You can make profits when the value of the fx pair goes down, and you will lose your investment if it rises. This pair will rise if the USD increases its price against the JPY. Therefore, it is actually a trust on the JPY.

Another alternative is to use futures and options, which are derivative products, so you can make money from the currency value changes. If you purchase a currency pair option, you can gain the privilege to buy a pair on a specific rate. Meanwhile, a futures forex contract could build the agreement to purchase the currency pair at a specific point.

These trading strategies are often employed by more experienced traders, but as a beginner, you should be at least aware of them.

Order Types

In looking for a new trading position, you may have to use a market order or a limit order, which are actually similar when you are placing a new position in the stock market.

A market order can provide you with the capacity to acquire the currency at a specific exchange rate that it is presently trading in the foreign exchange market. On the other hand, the limit order will allow you to identify a specific entry price.

If you are holding an open position in the market, you may have to consider employing a take profit order, so you could lock in your gains.

For instance, let us assume that you are sure that the USD/GBP will react at 1.8700, but you are not completely certain that the price will rise any higher. You can use a take-profit order that will immediately close your position if the price hits 1.8700, which will lock in your profits.

The stop loss order is also a tool that you can use when you want to hold the open positions. This will allow you to figure out if the price could decline prior to the closing of the position and more losses could be accumulated.

Hence, if the USD/GBP rate starts to drop, the investor may put a stop-loss, which could halt the position to avoid any further loss.

When you are also day trading in the stock market, you will realize that the order types that you could enter in the forex trading accounts are quite similar. It is crucial to be familiar with these orders before you actually place your very first trade in the foreign exchange market.

Chapter 9 - Day Trading ETFs and Options

Exchange-Traded Funds are financial securities that involve a collection of securities like equities or even currencies that usually monitor an underlying index.

ETFs also involve different sectors or industries and also use different strategies. In many ways, ETFs are like mutual funds. But they are listed on exchanges and the shares can also be traded by retail traders.

A popular ETF is the SPDR S&P 500 or simply known as SPY that monitors the S&P 500 Index. It contains different types of investments including bonds, commodities, and equities. Because ETFs are marketable securities, it has an associated price, which allows it to be traded.

ETFs also bring together in one instrument some of the paramount features offered by equities and mutual funds. Many ETFs seek to monitor a benchmark index, then trade shares on exchanges such as stock. They are also available for each major asset class such as stocks or equities, bonds or fixed income, cash, and commodities.

ETFs offer a more affordable alternative to obtain exposure to a group that otherwise would have been quite hard to trade.

For example, if you want to put your money in gold, you have different options. You may buy actual gold bars or coins, or you can try trading contracts for gold futures. But these are usually tedious and difficult methods.

The most affordable option here is to get gold ETF shares that follow gold's market price. You can do this with less effort and at a lot lower price. If you project that the whole stock market will rise, you can purchase a stock index such as Dow Jones. You may either purchase DJIA futures contracts or buy all the 30 companies that comprise the Dow Index.

If you like to do this for a cheaper alternative, you can easily purchase EFT shares that follow Dow Jones such as the DIA ETF.

Day traders generally love ETFs because of their high volatility. In this chapter, we will learn how you can trade ETF.

Retail trading is one of the most preferred ETF trading strategies due to its high market volatility. Therefore, day traders can buy & sell ETFs anytime throughout the day. There are different ETF platforms available, but the best ETF today are the following:

- iSHares MSCI Emerging Markets ETF

- ProShares UltraVIX ShortTerm Futures ETF (UVXY)

- Gold Miners ETF (GDX)

- ProShares VIX ShortTerm Futures ETF (UVXY)

- SPDR S&P 500 (SPY)

These are also part of the busiest ETF exchanges in the US. Day traders can take advantage of highly profitable short-term EFT opportunities. But the chances of making a profit by betting on day trading can be limited. This is the reason you have to carefully assess the rules in ETF trading.

Here are the specific steps in trading ETFs:

1. Select the Right Exchange Traded Funds for Day Trading

In the US, the first and the most popular ETF is the SPDR S&P500 ETF or SPY ETF. Day traders are attracted to trade in SPY because it has the biggest AUM and trading volume. The SPY ETF monitors how the world's most famous stock index, the S&P 500, performs.

The top ETFs in the US ranked by Forbes Magazine according to Assets (in billion dollars) are the following

- SPDR S&P 500 (SPY) - $254

- iShares Core S&P500 (IVV) - $146.7

- Vanguard Total Stock Market (VTI) - $94.6

- Vanguard S&P500 (VOO) - $88.2

- iShares MSCI EAFE (EFA) - $78.3

- Vanguard FTSE Developed Markets (VEA) $72.1

- Vanguard FTSE Emerging Markets (VWO) $65.9

- Invesco QQQ (QQQ) $62.1

It is fairly reasonable that most day traders choose SPY ETF as the prime exchange for their day trading. But you should not assume that all ETFs are the same since they are obviously not. If you are not certain which one you should trade, just opt for the most popular and most trusted exchange, which is SPY.

2. Use the 50-period MA (15-Minute Trend)

Among the most commonly used stock trading indicators is the 50-period moving average. This is actually a psychological indicator that many day traders use to analyze the sentiment in the ETF market.

The 50-period moving average is more relevant to the price movement because many traders use it. This is the main reason the 50 MA is used alongside the trading range opening.

The chart below shows the 50 MA in SPDR S&P 500

3. Jump into Trade after 10 AM Eastern Time

In day trading ETFs, it is ideal to concentrate on the starting trading range. The trading session in the morning is when smart money typically comes in, and also when the biggest volume happens.

So if you focus only on the AM session, you can avoid being stuck to the chart the entire day, and you can only trade alongside organizational investors.

SPDR S&P500 regularly starts trading at 9:30 AM Eastern Time. However, you should allocate the first half hour after the market opens to observe the trading patterns.

Day trading ETFs is mostly about trading the opportunities during the time of day that is most volatile.

4. Wait for the Price to Hold Over 50-Period MA and Open the Upper Portion of the past 5-day Trade

After analyzing how the market performs during the first half hour of the market session, you should find the price to keep over the key 50-period moving average.

Moreover, the SPDR S&P500 ETF also requires opening the upper half of the past five-day trading range. Just mark the past trading days as well as the peak price of the particular range.

Hold above the 50-period MA if you noticed that on the 6th day you open somewhere near the peak price.

5. Place Stop Loss (25 cents) under the 50-period MA

With this day trading strategy, you need to place your stop loss at 25 cents just under the 50-period MA.

If after the session, the market is breaking under the 50 MA, it means that the bears are getting stronger. Remember this indicator as it is key in making money in ETF day trading.

6. Get Your Profit if the SPY Advances a Dollar

This particular ETF day trading setup depends on the assumption that if each of the conditions above are met, then there's a high chance the SPY ETF will advance at least a dollar. Manually close the trade if you are not able to reach your target profit.

The chart above shows a good example of a buying trade. You can still follow similar rules for a selling trade, only in reverse order.

Day trading ETFs offers basic investment opportunities without investing too much on operating costs compared to equities and forex market. However, you can really make a lot of money as a day trader if you know how to leverage ETF's intraday high volatility.

Options Day Trading

Aside from stocks, forex, and futures, and ETFs. you can also day trade options, which are direct financial derivatives. Options are basically legal contracts that allow you to buy or sell an instrument during or within a pre-established date or exercise date.

If you are selling options, you need to fulfill the terms of the transactions. These could either be buy or sell if the buyer opts to exercise the option before the expiry date.

Day trading options can span across different markets. You may obtain equities options, forex options, ETF options, futures options, and more. These conventional options are also called 'vanilla options'.

Options Contract

If you own an options contract, you will be provided with a number of rights. The options contract includes the following details:

- Types of options (put or call)

- Underlying instrument (equities, bonds, etc.)

- Trade units (the number of shares)

- Strike price (the price at which you can exercise the option)

- Expiry date (the last day you can exercise the option)

Types of Options

Options are usually categorized as risky and complicated investments, and this places off different aspiring traders. There are two types of options:

- Call - These are buying options that will allow you to buy a stock at a certain price.

- Put - These are selling options that will allow you to sell a stock at a certain price.

Aside from the two primary classes, there's a long list of various markets and options available. While not all options are available for day trading, the list includes:

- Equities options

- Mini options

- Index options

- Crude oil options

- Futures options

- SPY Options

- E-Mini options

- QQQ options

- OEX options

- ETF options

- IRA options

- ES weekly options

More often than not, you will find that most options are based on stocks of publicly listed companies such as Amazon or Google. But there is also an increasing number of options based on alternative underlying instruments such as real estate investment trusts (REITs), commodities, currencies, and stock indexes.

If you are interested in day trading stock options, you need to understand that the contracts for these instruments are based on 100 shares of the stock. This rule is not applicable, however, if the adjustments occur as a result of mergers or stock splits.

Most ETF stock options are in the US, and can be exercised at any point between the buying date and expiry date. On the other hand, European options can only be redeemed on the expiry date.

As you learn different financial instruments, you may realize several similarities between options and day trading. These are often based on the same underlying instrument. The composition of the actual contracts also share several similarities.

The main difference is how you trade options and futures. In options, you will get a wider range of available vehicles. You will also find that the trading rules are different. You can trade options singularly or you can buy them alongside futures contracts or stocks to serve like trade insurance.

The Benefits of Day Trading Options

There are several reasons you can make huge profits in day trading options. But aside from financial rewards, day trading options usually has its own appeal to traders.

Low Cost Strategy

Day trading options will provide you with the opportunity to participate and get out in the market faster and with minimum risk compared to other financial instruments such as mutual funds or equities. It is also considerably more affordable to buy an option than to buy the underlying instruments such as shares. Therefore, you can control the same number of shares with minimum capital.

Diversity

Because options are a lot more affordable than purchasing the actual stock, you can take advantage of several opportunities for investments. Therefore, your capital can go further, which increases your potential for profit.

More Benefits for Day Traders

Once the security moves, the day trader can take advantage even more with an option. For example, if a stock moves from $30 to $60, this will bring you a 100% gain in shares. But a call option that moves from $2 per contract to $10 per contract will provide you with a 5x gain. Hence, you can earn more and faster with options.

Advantage over Other Securities

Options have the power to succeed where other financial securities often fail. While some securities fail, options can easily make you money. This is partly due to the fact that you don't need to exercise your option in order to make money. Moreover, high volatility is always attractive for making profits.

Mutually Beneficial for Buyers and Sellers

While options are usually built on stocks, they can give you better benefits if combined. This is due to the fact that you have the option to sell your options so you can create an income on the stocks that you are holding.

But like other financial instruments, day trading options has its own drawbacks. These include the following:

Price Movement Reductions

Price movement is often limited to the time value element of the premium options. In spite of the fact that the value may increase with the price of the underlying financial instrument, it can still be undermined by the loss of time value. But it is interesting to note that the time value for day trading options is relatively limited.

Wider Bid-Ask Spreads

If you compare it to stocks, the bid-ask spread is often wider in options day trading. This is often due to the lower liquidity often found in the options market. This may fluctuate as much as 50% that can further reduce your profit.

These downsides should not discourage you from trying day trading options. As long as you know how to trade and you have your own day trading plan, you can take advantage of income opportunity from options day trading.

Chapter 10 - Biggest Mistakes Beginners Make in Day Trading and How to Avoid Them

While you can make substantial gains from day trading in a single day, there is also the risk of losing all of your money in a single trade. This is especially true if you don't know how to use leverage for your advantage or commit specific ill-adviced practices that can end up draining your account.

There are common day trading mistakes that retail traders usually make in the hope of gaining high returns, but end up losing a lot of money. With knowledge, discipline, and alternative methodologies, you can avoid these trading mistakes.

Chasing Trades

A common mistake in day trading is chasing trades. Instead of focusing on stable and steady profits, some newbies are tempted to chase after fast-moving stocks. They borrow money from the brokerage more than they can afford.

This could wipe out your account. A lot of people who have chased trades and experienced substantial losses are the ones who usually give day trading a bad review. Chasing trades if day trading instruments shoot up could lead to losses. Avoid chasing stocks that you have missed. You will only hurt yourself if you try to chase a train that has started running.

Averaging Down

Beginners in day trading usually experience difficulty when it comes to averaging down. Most of these traders commit this mistake unintentionally. The primary concern with averaging down is not only can it cost you money. It can also cost time, which could otherwise be allocated for other trades that can provide you better returns.

Meanwhile, a higher return is required on the remaining fund in order to initiate replenishment. If you lose half of your capital, it will require 100% return in order to gain back your capital to its original level. Losing huge chunks of capital on a single day or on a single trade can easily cripple the growth of your capital in time.

While averaging down may work on special circumstances, this strategy will eventually result in a margin call or substantial loss because a trend can only sustain itself depending on your liquidity.

News Prepositioning

While you may be aware of certain news events that can influence the market, the direction is still uncertain. You might even be confident about the possible news such as political activities that can affect a sector or an industry, but there is no way to accurately project how the market will behave after the news. There are also added indicators behind the news announcements, which could make the movement highly illogical yet possible.

All sorts of orders can also hit the market and stops could be triggered on different sides of the trade. This usually leads to a back and forth action prior to the emergence of a trend. Taking a position prior to a news announcement can substantially damage your chances of winning the trade.

Quick Trading after News Announcement

A news announcement hits the market and the market players start to react. At first, it seems like a no-brainer to ride the bandwagon so you can take advantage of the market sentiment. If you do this without a plan and without a formidable trading strategy, you may end up losing the trade.

News releases usually result in fluctuation in the market mainly because of hair-pin turns and lack of liquidity in the market assessment of the report. There are even trades that are in the money but would end up quickly turning and bringing large losses as significant swings happen.

Liquidity is crucial for these times, which could mean that losses can probably be much more than expected. Successful traders usually wait for some time for the volatility to subside, so there will be a definitive trend after the hype.

Trading More than 2% of Your Capital in a Single Trade

Take note that higher risk doesn't always mean higher returns. Most traders who risk huge amounts of money on a single trade will typically lose in the long term.

A common rule of the thumb is that you should only risk a maximum of 2 per cent of your capital on one trade. If you have accumulated enough experience and skills in forex trading, you can increase your limit to 3 per cent.

You must also establish a daily maximum risk, which for beginners, can be 2 % of the capital or equal to the average daily profit in a month. For instance, if you have $50,000 in your account (without the leverage), you should not lose $1,000 in a single day.

With this strategy, you can make certain that no single day of trading or single trade could affect the account substantially.

Not Understanding Financial Markets

Regardless of the financial instrument that you choose to day trade - stocks, currencies, or ETFs, you need to really understand the market.

For example, there's always a toss-up between a limit and market order. While the limit order allows establishment of maximum or minimum price for trading securities, the market order is an order to buy or sell instruments at prevailing market rates.

While market orders could be filled quickly, the market has no ability to control the order. Likewise, limit orders can allow the parameters to be regulated. Whether market orders or limit orders make sense to you, you have to understand that you can't miss a fast-paced stock to save a few dollars.

High-quality instruments that are naturally liquid allow the use of either limit order or market order.

Unrealistic Projections

Regardless of your dreams or goals in day trading, the market is insensitive to what you expect. Before you even start trading, you should accept the fact that the financial markets could be illogical and volatile.

In order to avoid disappointments from unrealistic expectations, you should have a trading plan and stick to this strategy when you are doing the actual trade. If the results are steady, still stick to your trade plan. In the forex market, even a minor gain could become substantial in the long run.

As your fund grows over time, the position size could be increased so you can bring in higher returns. Also, if you want to test a new strategy, you should only do so with minimal capital. You can allocate more capital into a strategy if you see positive results.

The financial markets are also quite volatile near the open. You can use certain strategies in the opening, which are not ideal near the closing. The market may become more stable as the day progresses, and there may be a pickup in action towards the close that may require another form of strategy. The key in this fluctuating market is to accept what is provided by the market and don't expect too much from the system.

Relying Too Much on Day Trading Insights Found Online

Learning the fundamentals of day trading is crucial. Exploring proven day trading strategies is also essential. However, as you practice in this career, you need to develop your own strategy.

Nowadays, there is a lot of 'day trading tips' that you can read online. But there's no guarantee that all of them can help you become a successful day trader. It is best to cut through the noise, and learn how to find your own voice. Just remember the day trading process that we have discussed in Chapter 7.

Chapter 11 - The Importance of Continuous Education in Day Trading

Success in day trading is largely based on three essential skills:

1. **Critical Analysis** - you have to assess the tension between sellers and buyers and place your money in the winning group

2. **Financial Management** - You need to practice excellent money management or else you will lose your money in no time

3. **Self-Discipline** - You need to be highly disciplined and stick to your trading plan. You have to avoid getting overly depressed or excited in the financial markets and the temptation to make decisions based on your emotions.

Now after reading this book, you must be in a better position to decide whether or not day trading is really the right career for you. Remember, day trading requires a specific mindset, discipline, and a set of skills that you need to improve in the long run.

It is interesting to take note that many successful day traders are also avid players of poker. They say that they enjoy the stimulation and speculation that comes from this game.

But you need to remember that poker is a type of gambling. Day trading is not because it dwells on the realm of science. It requires skill, discipline, and other skills that have nothing to do with luck like gambling.

Selling and buying financial instruments is a serious business. You must be able to make quick decisions, with no hesitation or emotion. Doing otherwise could lead to a substantial loss of money and also depression in some individuals who don't yet have a formidable mind.

Once you have made up your mind and you have finally decided that you like to begin day trading, the next step is to be properly educated. You must never begin your career in day trading using actual cash. Look for brokers that will allow you to play with simulated accounts but are using real market data.

There are some day trading brokers who will offer access to an account that uses delayed market data. This is not the best simulator to use. You have to work with real-time data so you can make actual decisions.

The majority of simulated data software are premium tools, so you have to save money for this software. Avoid free trials as many of them are cheap platforms. Remember, if you pay peanuts, you get monkeys. Invest in your education, and education in day trading requires an upfront cost.

For instance, let's say that you want to get your master's degree. This goal will easily cost you around $40,000 or even more. Similarly, many diploma or post-graduation programs will cost a lot more compared to the education needed for your day trading career.

When you have a simulated account, you need to develop your own strategy. Try the day trading strategies we have explored in this book. Ideally, you should become a master of one strategy. Reversal Strategies, Resistance or Support, and VWAP are the easiest day trading strategies.

You only have to master a few day trading strategies so you become profitable in this career. Keep it simple. Once you have mastered a strong strategy, make certain that you detach your emotions when you do the trade.

Continue practicing with the level of money that you will trade in an actual account. It can be easy to purchase a position worth $50,000 in a simulated platform and watch 50% of it vanish in a matter of minutes. However, do you have the tolerance to lose this amount of money in real life?

If your answer is no, then you will probably become too emotional while you are trading, and make quick decisions that will ultimately result in substantial loss. Therefore, always trade with the position and size that you will also use in an actual account. Otherwise, it makes no sense to trade in a simulator.

You can move to a real account after training with a simulator and then begin with small real cash. Limit the number of your trades if you are still learning or you feel that you are not emotionally prepared. Continue your self-education, and be sure to reflect on your trading strategy.

Do not stop learning about day trading and the market you want to participate in - equities, forex, ETFs, or futures. These financial markets are quite dynamic. Day trading is quite different than it was a decade ago, and it will be different in another decade.

So continue reading and discussing your performance and progress with other day traders. Learn how to think ahead and keep a progressive attitude. Read as much as you can, but still keep a level of skepticism about everything you encounter, including this book, of course.

Ask important questions, and don't accept 'expert insights' at face value. Ideally, you should join a group or community of day traders. It can be extremely difficult to trade alone.

It can also be emotionally overwhelming. It will help you a lot if you are part of a community of day traders so you can ask questions, discuss options, learn new strategies, and receive alerts and hints about the financial markets. But don't forget that you also need to contribute.

It is essential to take note, however, that if you are part of a community of day traders, you must not always follow the pack. Try to become an independent thinker.

In general, people do change once they become part of a crowd. They become more impulsive, unquestioning, and always looking for a 'guru' whose trades they can follow. They respond with the crowd rather than using their own minds.

Day trading groups may receive some trends together but could lose if the trends reverse. Don't forget that profitable day traders know how to think on their own. Learn how to use your judgment when to pursue the trade, and when to get out.

Conclusion

Thanks again for taking the time to read this book!

By now, you should have a good understanding of day trading and the different financial markets that you can trade. Hopefully, the lessons you have learned in this beginner's guide will help you to decide if this is really a good career for you.

As a recap, I would like you to remember the following day trading rules that we have discussed in this book:

> ***Rule No. 1*** *- Day trading is not a get-rich-quick scheme.*

> ***Rule No. 2*** *- Day trading is hard.*

> ***Rule No. 3*** *- Do not hold stocks overnight.*

> ***Rule No. 4*** *- Always ask: is this stock moving because the general market is moving, or there's a unique catalyst behind this movement?*

> ***Rule No. 5*** *- Risk management is important for successful day trading.*

> ***Rule No. 6*** *- Your broker will trade the stocks for you.*

Rule No. 7 - Day traders only trade apex predators.

Rule No. 8 - Filled candlesticks signify selling pressure, hollow candlesticks indicate buying pressure.

Rule No. 9 - Technical indicators will only guide you. They should not dictate you.

Rule No. 10 - Don't allow your emotions to cloud your judgment.

You can print these rules and pin it near where you perform your trade. This will allow you to make a quick reference.

Although this book is only a small slice of all you can learn about day trading, I hope that you have gained enough insights into this topic to have the confidence to get started in your trading journey.

I also encourage you to learn more about the intricacies and the complexities of each financial instrument that you are interested to trade. You should also continue exploring the best strategies so you can find this career worthy of your time and talent.

Thanks again, and good luck.

Thank you

Before you go, I just wanted to say thank you for purchasing my book.

You could have picked from dozens of other books on the same topic but you took a chance and chose this one.

So, a HUGE thanks to you for getting this book and for reading all the way to the end.

Now I wanted to ask you for a small favor. **Could you please consider posting a review on the platform? Reviews are one of the easiest ways to support the work of authors.**

This feedback will help me continue to write the type of books that will help you get the results you want. So if you enjoyed it, please let me know.

References

Bull Flag Chart Pattern & Trading Strategies - Warrior Trading. (2019, September 24). Retrieved November 11, 2019, from https://www.warriortrading.com/bull-flag-trading/

Day Trading Options - Rules, Strategy and Brokers for intraday options trading. (n.d.). Retrieved November 9, 2019, from https://www.daytrading.com/options

Floating Stock Definition and Example. (2019, October 6). Retrieved November 11, 2019, from https://www.investopedia.com/terms/f/floating-stock.asp

Forex Market Definition. (2019, May 4). Retrieved November 11, 2019, from https://www.investopedia.com/terms/forex/f/forex-market.asp

How Is the Exponential Moving Average (EMA) Formula Calculated? (n.d.). Retrieved November 11, 2019, from https://www.investopedia.com/ask/answers/122314/what-exponential-moving-average-ema-formula-and-how-ema-calculated.asp

How to use doji candlestick patterns. (n.d.). Retrieved November 11, 2019, from https://blog.liquid.com/doji-candlestick-patterns

Institutional Traders vs. Retail Traders: What's the Difference? (2019, April 10). Retrieved November 11, 2019, from https://www.investopedia.com/articles/active-trading/030515/what-difference-between-institutional-traders-and-retail-traders.asp

Live, I. (2016, June 14). The Chart Pattern That Made Me Over $100,000 in Trading Profits. Retrieved November 11, 2019, from https://www.investorsunderground.com/the-chart-pattern-that-made-me-over-100000-in-trading-profits/

Make Money Day Trading Despite the Challenges. (2019, August 27). Retrieved October 18, 2019, from https://www.thebalance.com/why-it-is-so-hard-to-make-consistent-money-day-trading-1031238

Malik, P. (2019, August 28). Top 3 Simple Moving Average Trading Strategies. Retrieved November 11, 2019, from https://tradingsim.com/blog/simple-moving-average

Reversal Day Trading Strategies for Beginners | Warrior Trading. (2019, October 15). Retrieved November 11, 2019, from https://www.warriortrading.com/reversal-trading-strategy/

Risk Management. (2017, May 25). Retrieved November 11, 2019, from https://www.thebalance.com/day-trading-risk-management-4073426

Simple Moving Average (SMA) Definition. (n.d.). Retrieved November 9, 2019, from https://www.investopedia.com/terms/s/sma.asp

Trader, M. (2013, June 6). Sharks, Whales and Apex Predators. Retrieved November 11, 2019, from https://www.businessinsider.com/sharks-whales-and-apex-predators-2013-6?international=true&r=US&IR=T

Using Bullish Candlestick Patterns To Buy Stocks. (2019, June 25). Retrieved November 11, 2019, from https://www.investopedia.com/articles/active-trading/062315/using-bullish-candlestick-patterns-buy-stocks.asp

Volume Weighted Average Price (VWAP) Definition. (n.d.). Retrieved November 11, 2019, from https://www.investopedia.com/terms/v/vwap.asp

Williams, J. (2019, October 11). 4 Best Indicators for Swing Trading and Tips.... Retrieved November 11, 2019, from https://ragingbull.com/swing-trading/back-basics-day-trading-vs-swing-trading/